Wonderful Ways
TO BE
A FAMILY

JUDY
FORD

Wonderful Ways

TO **BE**

A FAMILY

Foreword by
Susan Isaacs Kohl, author of
The Best Things Parents Do

Conari
Press

This edition first published in 2006 by
Red Wheel/Weiser, LLC
With offices at:
500 Third Street, Suite 230
San Francisco, CA 94107
www.redwheelweiser.com

ISBN-10: 1-57324-295-0
ISBN-13: 978-1-57324-295-0

Library of Congress Cataloging-in-Publication Data

Ford, Judy, 1944–
Wonderful ways to be a family/Judy Ford
p.   cm.
ISBN 1-57324-124-5 (alk. paper)
1. Family. 2. Parenting.   I. Title.
HQ518.F67   1998
306.85—dc21   98-6517

Typeset in Bembo by Maija Tollefson

Printed in Canada

TCP

10 9   8 7 6 5 4 3 2 1

Your family waited
for you to arrive
and was there to greet you.

Hopefully, when you die
they'll be at your bedside.

In the meantime
it's the gestures you make,
the actions you take
that matter.

It's your capacity to be
loving and lighthearted
that makes you a family.

Wonderful Ways to Be a Family

Celebrate with One Another

Cherish One Another

An Enormous Bag of Skills

Families—an overwhelming topic. Traditional family, nontraditional family, extended family, absence of family, family of man—all crowd and dance together in my mind. As I think about the topic, I'm sure of one thing: a harmonious family is possible, must be possible, because a family provides the best opportunity for everyone in it to grow.

This book is about you and the people you call family. You and your family are interdependent; as the stars are related to the moon, as the moon is related to the universe, so you're connected to one another. By divine design your lives are linked, interwoven. You need each other for reasons that aren't always clear, but are always compelling.

Our families help us get through life. When you're a child, your family provides you food and shelter, teaches you the ropes, loves and protects you. When you're an adult, your family adds meaning and purpose to your life. As an elder looking back on where you've been, you have a sense of history, of evolution; you can see how far you've come. It's in the hearts of your loved ones that you live on.

Families come in a wide configuration, composed of a myriad of possibilities: married folks with no children, married parents, single parents, step-parents, chosen children, half brothers and sisters, grandparents, foster children, a spiritual brother, friends living together, a single person living alone with a close confidante down the street—all with a few dogs, cats, or a goldfish or two. These days, the nuclear family is not the only arrangement, and family values are not just evident in traditional families. Single parents are doing a fine job, as are adoptive nonrelated parents. What's important is the sense of relatedness you feel toward one another, not the particular form your family takes.

Being a member of a family, no matter its form, has many dimensions to it. It's a big responsibility. You're in each other's lives both to teach and learn about what it means to be human—hopefully, human in the loveliest way. It's not easy to be a member of a family because it's not always apparent who is the teacher and who is the student. My experience is that you're both—often at the same time. (During family struggles, it might be helpful to remember this.) You'll face difficulties, challenges, and unpleasantness at every stage. You'll have to figure out how to share the bathroom, the closets, and the car with people who often share the same last name, yet on some days seem like strangers. You'll have emotional upheavals.

Navigating your way through the complex feelings that arise when you're dependent on each other can be like walking through a brier patch. You'll have to face each other and that can be prickly. Relationships with parents can be particularly touchy. For a portion of your life you couldn't survive without these people feeding you, clothing you, giving you shelter; if that's not enough to make you panic, there's the undeniable fact that biologically (unless you're adopted) you come from the same gene pool, which has certain consequences. Acquaintances have told you "You look just like your Mother," or "You have your Grandfather's nose." Try though you might, you can't deny it—you're related. Spiritually your lives are interwoven as well; you've been brought together to fulfill a higher purpose, which in moments of anguish, you'll yearn to discover.

Creating a happy and healthy family requires an enormous bag of skills. When your child is a baby, it seems as if you pack the entire house just to run an errand or go to the grocery store. You carry a big diaper bag with lots of paraphernalia including diapers, a pacifier, bottles of juice, formula, a change of clothing, a bib, a blanket, a rattle, a toy or two, baby food, and a plastic container of Cheerios. When the baby cries, you reach into the diaper bag for what you think might calm the baby. You change diapers, and that might work or it might not. If the baby still fusses, you try something else, perhaps the pacifier or a bottle; again, that might work or might not. Sometimes the first thing you try satisfies the baby perfectly, other times no matter what you do nothing works, and you end up eating the Cheerios yourself. As your little ones grow out of babyhood, you exchange your diaper bag for an invisible bag of skills. They don't need bottles and diapers anymore, now they do need continual guidance—guidance cloaked with love and laughter. The more skills you have in your invisible bag the better equipped you'll be. Sometimes it's a bit of advice that's needed, other times heart talks do the trick, and in between you have to put your foot down and say "no." It's complicated because what works one day may not work the next; what works for one child may not work for the second. That's why the more skills you have, the happier you'll be.

Being a family member is more than being a parent. And it takes just as many skills to be a loving daughter to your dying father, to not blow up when your mother criticizes your haircut for the 4000th time, and to negotiate between your parents and his as to where to have Thanksgiving dinner. Whatever your family situation, it asks you to learn, to grow, to mature spiritually and emotionally.

Based on the principles of love and laughter, *Wonderful Ways to Be a Family* is a prescription for sustaining the family you've got—with all their quirks and annoying habits. It's not about improving you or your family; it's not about trading them in for another one; it's not about dysfunction. Heaven knows, all families have their own peculiar brand of dysfunction. Rather, *Wonderful Ways to Be a Family* is about increasing the love and laughter that holds a family together. It's about creating the warm feelings that togetherness brings. It's about tuning into each other's wavelength so that whatever time you do spend together uplifts your spirit. It's about laughing, crying, and loving. It's about being a member of a far-from-perfect, human family.

Family life is a journey of love, of self-discovery, of sacrifice, and of celebration. It's not a quick or easy trek, but it will bring you unmeasured joy. It's worth it, because through it all, you'll grow into a happy, loving, mature person who can proudly say, "These are my people."

Living with Love and Laughter Quiz

(Answer yes or no)

1. My children (and/or parents) know what kind of music I like.
2. I make sure to include something fun in every day.
3. I make a special point of hanging out with my family each week.
4. I am silly at least ten minutes each day.
5. When asked about my past, I tell the truth.
6. When I'm with my family the television is off more than it is on.
7. I call my family by special love names.
8. If I start a new project, I'll let myself quit after a short time if I'm sure I don't like it.
9. I let my kids stay home from school once in a while even if they aren't sick.
10. I play hooky once in awhile from work.
11. My family views me as a fun person.
12. I read books for relaxation.
13. My family has seen me dance.
14. I do a physical activity each week.
15. My home life is relaxed.
16. I am able to see the positive side when things go wrong.
17. I cry in front of my family.

18. I know how to express anger without dumping on others.

19. I am able to negotiate with my children and/or parents when we disagree.

20. I accept feedback from my spouse, children, and/or parents.

21. I laugh with my children daily.

22. I laugh with my partner daily.

23. I think my children have something important to teach me.

24. We eat dinner together at least three times a week and enjoy it.

25. I give my children unexpected treats or awards just because.

26. I surprise my family with unexpected gifts.

27. We acknowledge small accomplishments.

28. I can keep messes in perspective.

29. Our family traditions add meaning and pleasure to our lives.

30. I make sure to say "I love you" to the important people in my life.

31. I have told my parents how much they mean to me.

32. I show respect for my elders.

33. I smile at babies.

34. I make a conscious effort to smile directly at my child each day.

35. I am able to listen to my child for one minute without offering advice, interrupting, or asking questions.

36. My child has heard me sing.

37. I have taught my child to whistle.

38. I take a lighthearted approach when solving problems.

39. I am able to show affection to family members.

40. I am interested in my spouse and show it.

41. I whistle while doing chores around the house.

42. When I've blown it, I will apologize to family members.

43. I spend time each day doing something I love.

44. I spend time with my children each day doing something we all enjoy.

45. I am able to say "no" without feeling guilty and without lecturing.

46. I am able to stay calm and laugh about small disruptions.

47. I am able to give strong directives without yelling.

48. My kids respect me more than they fear me.

49. I can laugh at my own mistakes.

50. When I'm impatient with my children I remind myself that they have not been on the earth very long.

51. I am enthusiastic and cheerful.

52. I enjoy my family every day.

53. My family knows that they are my top priority.

54. I am optimistic.

55. I avoid name-calling, criticism, and put-downs.

56. I put my focus on what my kids are doing right.

57. I put my focus on what I am doing right.

58. At the end of the day, I am able to put events in perspective and begin fresh in the morning.

59. My family would describe me as positive and loving.

60. I feel like I am living with friends: people I like and trust.

61. Our home is comfortable and cozy.

62. Our home is safe.

63. The people in my family are relaxed and cheerful most of the time.

64. Our family is able to talk about what is troubling us.

65. We take downtime for loafing, hanging out, and puttering around.

Total number of yes answers: _____

Scoring

(The total number of yes answers.)

0-10   Your family life is much too serious. You're probably not enjoying yourself and you're having difficulty relaxing. Perhaps you didn't have much fun growing up. You can change that pattern now by putting your focus on enjoying your family. You need to heal the wounds of your own childhood.

11-21   Your family life is tense, and so are you. You're worried, anxious, and under pressure. This is affecting your family. You need to find healthy ways to relax and unwind. Remember: Don't sweat the small stuff. Focus on having fun. Make a daily practice of smiling directly at your children and spouse each day.

22-32   Your family life is moving in a good direction. You're beginning to enjoy your children. You understand that children respond well to kindness. Let yourself and your children be silly. Find ways to play together.

33-44   Your family life is important to you, and you are able to focus on what truly matters in life. Remember it's the quality of your relationship with your family that matters in the long run. Hang out together without the pressures of doing. Listen more.

45-55   Your parenting style is upbeat, and your children are able to laugh with you. Keep it up by adding a little more laughter each day.

56-65   You live in a nurturing family. Your parenting style is positive. Your children are developing good self-esteem. Keep doing what you're doing because you are on the right track.

Foreword

In this expanding age when the word family takes on new definitions almost daily, Judy Ford explores the issues that make a difference in the quality of our lives. Our links with people are no longer defined by biological ties that make us feel separate from others—our name, our territory, our clan. Today, family works when the threads that connect us contain the experience of love. Whether parents are a man and a woman, a single woman or man, or two women or men, raising children works well when the people involved expand their abilities to create love. They don't just talk about love but learn to bring about the actual experience.

In our materialistic society, we know everything about helping a child achieve. Parents are overloaded with information on making their children feel superior to others. In the book you hold in your hands, Ford offers us concrete ways to teach children how to develop their capacities for kindness, caring, or cooperation; to help them feel worthy of love and able to share the fruits of their loving experiences with others. Competing with others creates the modern angst of loneliness and lack of belonging, hence going along with the crowd. Wonderful Ways to Be a Family shows us how to create the opposite—the kind of connection that fosters feelings of unity, first with family, then with all of life.

The expanded definitions of family exemplified in this book show us that, with a foundation of love, families can honor and celebrate divergent personalities and points of view. What could be mor important for ushering in the light of new generations to come! In my everyday experience consulting with parents and families, I can't think of any learning that we need more.

—**Susan Isaacs Kohl**, author of *The Best Things Parents Do*

Help One Another

A harmonious family is possible.
It should be your goal, because
it provides the best opportunity
for everyone to grow.

Provide a Safe Haven

The very first thing that you can do for your family is to provide a safe place to be together—a resting spot, a peaceful sanctuary, a home. It doesn't matter if your safe haven is a mansion with a private bathroom for every person or a small apartment with one tiny bath. The only absolute requirement is that your home be safe. A place where, at the beginning and end of each day, family members gather to relax, put their feet up, and let their hair down, knowing that they're surrounded by people who care and in whom they can trust.

Your home is your collective retreat from the world where each of you can restore your soul and renew your energy so that everyone—young or old—has the vigor, spunk, and eagerness to face another day.

Your home should be clean, but not necessarily neat. Active families are doing things, and wherever there are kids and pets, artists and geniuses, at work and at play, there's bound to be clutter and dust balls. Organization and neatness are handy but a comfortable home full of positive energy will serve your family best. Especially for many women, it's easy to get so caught up in cleaning that we lose all sense of fun. A safe haven wraps you in contentment. It's filled with light and color, not designed as a showplace to impress, but arranged for enjoyment and activity.

For a home to be safe you must create an atmosphere free from tension, worry, put-downs, and hostilities. It must be free from anger, depression, ridicule, emotional blackmail, and physical threats. That doesn't mean it will be conflict free, but with an attitude of acceptance, conflicts can be resolved in a spirit of cooperation. Each person knows that they matter, that they can speak up, and that their point of view will be heard. They look happy. They have smiling eyes and relaxed bodies. In a safe home every person is important and knows it.

A safe haven is filled with books, music, crayons, and paper. There are toys in the corner and backpacks piled on the floor. A safe haven is filled with movement and motion. There's laughter, dancing, and horsing around. Skates, bikes, scooters, balls, bats, teddy bears, and dolls are appropriate trimmings.

In a safe haven, each person contributes to personalizing the space. Especially when kids have a say in designing their rooms, choosing the colors, arranging their furniture, and choosing the pictures, they have a personal investment in keeping it comfortable. Mementos of family outings, children's drawings, a baby bonnet, and a bulletin board all add to the decor.

Take an inventory of your home environment. What impression does it make? Is it cozy, lively, and safe? Or do you feel apprehensive in it? Can you put your feet up? Or are your standards so unrealistic that you're always doing household chores? Remind yourself that you can have your home as neat as you like when your nest is empty, but for your own sanity and for the well-being of your family, for now creative clutter is best. It doesn't matter if you have lush carpets or garage-sale furnishings; it doesn't matter if you have fine china or mix-and-match plasticware; what does matter is that it feels good to walk through your front door!

Commit Yourself Completely

To be part of a loving family takes commitment—an enormous commitment, because you have no idea of what you're committing to or what might be asked of you in the future. In the beginning, the pledge seems easy and it comes naturally; after all, you love the other person, and you both want to be a family. But when family life gets a little rocky, as it surely will, you'll might question the wisdom of your original intention. You'll stand at a crossroads where you have to choose once again between venturing on your own or staying connected.

To be a member of a loving, lively family calls for your devotion, dedication, loyalty, and staunch determination. It's a commitment of heart and soul, not for the sake of the other family members alone, but for your own sake as well.

If it's a loving family you desire, you can't take an inactive role, you can't assume a passive attitude, you can't adopt a do-nothing posture. On the contrary, you'll put your family first, not because you have to, but because your commitment is all consuming and you find joy in doing so. The reward is an attachment so freeing that even when you're separated, you're still connected just the same.

The commitment I'm asking you to make is not a spoken one, not a public formal pledge. We all know that such commitments are easily broken. This commitment is much more subtle, unspoken, implied yet present just the same. It's a heart commitment made a thousand times over and stronger than a legal contract. At the end of a busy work day when you feel like putting your feet up and reading a book, for example, your commitment to your family means you put aside your desire for solitude and cook dinner.

Since few of us can predict the future, you're making this commitment without an inkling of what challenges you'll face, what burdens you'll bear, what victories you'll share. Yet in the darkness of not knowing, your commitment automatically arises, and you say to yourself, "This is my family; forever."

Your commitment arises from love. It contains a depth and totality of focus. Love first and commitment follows. If love disappears, your commitment is shaky.

To be part of a loving family and stay committed, you must keep love alive, fresh, ever flowing. Your behavior is the public affirmation of your pledge. How you treat your family matters; your attitude, each and every day, counts. Your commitment shines through your actions. If your loved ones let you down, don't snarl at them, accuse them, intentionally hurt them, turn your back, or walk away. Always treat them lovingly; put their best interest in the forefront of your mind. When you do, your reward is an indestructible bond that holds you together. Loving one another has that quality of commitment and continuity in it. If you want your family to be committed to you, be loving toward them.

Create a Team Identity

One of the unspoken tasks of a family is to assure each other that "we're a special, unique, one-of-a-kind, better-than-your-average" family. Creating family identity bolsters family esteem, which gives each person a lasting sense of belonging, pride, and wholeness. Jean explains how this phenomenon worked in her family:

"From an early age, I remember my mother saying, 'We're not like the average family,' and it was true. I see now that we may have been somewhat dysfunctional, but at the time, by the way my mother said it, as well as what I felt, I took it to mean we were special. Special as in, 'a cut above,' 'grade A,' 'prime.' I got this message from both my parents. My father was mostly absent and my mother was gifted in the art of denial, but as a child I believed I was blessed by my lot in life."

In the olden days, families proudly displayed a coat of arms or an emblem of their ancestry. When a couple marries, wedding rings are the outward symbol of the lifelong pledge they're making. You might consider choosing a symbol or designing a family logo to represent your commitment to one another. My daughter Amanda drew a picture of us when she was five years old. I liked it so much that I transferred it onto stationery and homemade greeting cards. Even though she's nineteen years old now, I still use it on note cards as a representation of our relationship. A client of mine made her son a quilt composed of family memories. She incorporated fish because fishing is their favorite pastime, two dogs that looked just like their pets, and other significant designs. She liked it so much she made one for herself. When other family members saw the quilts, they hinted so much that she made them quilts of their own. It's become a family tradition and each relative displays theirs proudly. The quilts increase their connection. Your family might wear baseball hats or t-shirts printed with a family crest you've chosen. You might find a lucky charm and hang it over your front door, paste it on the refrigerator door, or paint one over the fireplace.

To create a distinct family identity, you must talk about what it means to be a family and how special you are to each other, and reinforce it by sensitive displays of love, affection, and tender care. Ask yourselves: What does it mean to be part of our family? Think about a family motto. What would yours be? Talk about your family's purpose. What are your goals? What do you want to emphasize in your family? What you think about your family has far-reaching consequences. If you say out loud, "We're a family that likes each other," soon it will become a self-fulfilling prophecy.

Choose a Cooperative Parenting Style

There's great joy in cooperative parenting. Achieving it requires getting along with your partner, communicating about the nitty-gritty of daily life, and being cognizant of each other's weaknesses so that you can call on one another's strengths. Since you're not automatically going to think, feel, or act the same way, cooperative parenting involves appreciating your differences so that you can fully enjoy your togetherness and parent constructively. By combining your styles and maximizing your strengths, you'll get double the pleasure—the pleasure of happy children and the pleasure of working in unison with your sweetheart.

In my "Parenting with Love and Laughter" workshops, parents talk about what they like and dislike about parenting. You're not expected to like everything, you're not expected to always agree, nor are you expected to do it all well, but by combining your temperaments and natural inclinations, you make the job easier and get more enjoyment out of it.

The dynamics between parents have a lot to do with the child's behavior, so if you're cooperating well with each other, they'll reflect that back to you. By separating the tasks you enjoy and are good at from the ones you don't like or have to clench your teeth to get through, you can rely on one another to pick up the slack. "Lou likes to read bedtime stories and I don't," says Leah. "He's good at serving soup, nursing aches and pains, coaching Little League, and grocery shopping.

I'm good at helping with homework, making our home cozy, negotiating, listening, wiping runny noses, and making suggestions."

Parenting works best when you're open to your partner's approach, when you're able to see family life from his or her perspective, and when you accept feedback without getting defensive. Bouncing parenting issues around is handy, especially when what you're doing isn't getting the results you want. You can say, "Honey, what do you think about letting Susie go to the all-night party?" or "Do you think I was too harsh?" or "How do you suggest I might handle that differently?"

A cooperative parenting style is not for tyrants who flaunt their power or for martyrs who control by dumping guilt. It's about being an empowered, inspiring leader to your children and each other. It's about being loving, realistic, and lighthearted, trusting each other when you've gone off course. "He cautions me when I'm lecturing," says Helena, "and I warn him when his temper is on the verge of being out of control."

Do you emphasize your strengths? What are your weaknesses? What positive attributes do you bring to parenting? What areas do you need to learn more about? Cooperative parenting is seeing normal, everyday difficulties in new light. You can make many decisions in unison, but once in a while you'll need a chairman of the board. That's when you can trade off, depending on who is better at what.

Lead with Integrity

Integrity is pure and simple honesty. Living with integrity means getting to know yourself, inside and out, and communicating in a sincere, tactful manner. It means being willing to be open, and let your children, your spouse, and other family members see who you really are by giving them clear information about you. Leading with integrity means that you're not only willing to answer truthfully, but that your life is based on truth, you've stopped sneaking and hiding, and you're no longer pretending. You're living in the light, standing on a platform of truth. Living truthfully, being authentic, speaking honestly from your heart, is the basis for trust. Dishonesty destroys confidence and creates confusion, while honesty creates a firm foundation on which family life can be built.

Children learn about integrity through watching you lead your life. Do you practice what you preach? Are you genuine, upright, sincere? Are you living a respectable life? Does what you do match up with what you say? Do you know what goes on inside you? Or do you hide behind a mask, pretending you're something you're not?

Children learn lessons of honesty and integrity when you share your experience. Admit it, you've been cagey and devious some time in your life too. Shaming or punishing your children may teach them not to tell a lie about breaking the window, but it doesn't help them learn how to apply the "honesty is best" policy in other situations. You want them to understand the concept so that they can apply it to all parts of their lives.

Allow for Upset

In general, it's not safe in our culture to show upset. That's why there's so much interest in it. The media is rampant with stories about people who have gone to extreme measures to be heard: mowing down kids in a school, ramming someone with a car. We're alarmed, yet we watch with interest, wondering how one person could be filled with such rage. How does a person growing up in a family become so disturbed? Perhaps it's because they were upset for years and no one heard. Eventually, like a volcano, unable to keep the steam and lava inside, they blow. But fortunately you don't have to let it go that far. When you face upsets as they come, they won't pile up or cause explosions.

Upset is natural and can be an opportunity to understand yourself and your loved ones better. Even in the best of relationships, feelings fluctuate back and forth—sometimes we're in a love fest; other times we are angry with one another. Strong families know that conflicts and disagreements are part of any relationship. It's how you handle them that matters. Being upset is not bad as long as you face it. Indeed, upset lets you know that something needs fixing or changing. If you're upset there's likely to be a reason for it. When you uncover the source, you're no longer agitated. You're able to take positive steps, make changes, think clearly, and take action.

Sometimes the reason for your upset is obvious—the family pet dies, your in-laws have overstayed their welcome, you watch one of those sentimental commercials and are homesick for your family who lives a thousand miles away. Other times you might be upset but not sure why or what to do about it. If you're not sure, first focus your attention inward. Ask yourself, "What's going on with me right now?" Write your answers in a journal. After you've written about your upsets, you'll be more ready to talk them over. If your upset involves a family member, go to him or her and ask if you can talk about what's bothering you. If it doesn't involve anyone else, you still might want to talk it over anyway because being listened to is often all that's needed.

Families often jump too quickly into solving the problem before they know what the real problem is. Listening without interrupting, freaking out, offering advice, or criticizing lets the person get what's been bothering them off their chest and empowers them to come up with their own solution. Asking: "What are you going to do?" or "Is there anything you'd like me to do?" encourages them to confront their dilemmas.

When children are upset, parents usually try to make everything better. While that might resolve the immediate issue, it doesn't teach children problem solving. Instead, listening as they find their own solutions helps them build confidence and boost their self-awareness. Don't be afraid of their upsets because that is the beginning of problem solving.

A good rule of thumb to remember is that when you see that your child or spouse is upset, what they need more than anything else is "a good listening to."

Talk About What's Troubling You

We all at one time or another have suffered from the bad habit of answering, "I'm fine," when we really weren't so chipper. Maybe that's because we think we're complaining when we volunteer that we're down in the dumps, worried, or feeling blue. Maybe we think that no one would be interested. Maybe we don't want to be a pest, thinking we would be a nuisance to share our troubles. Maybe we think that it's better to think positively and that sharing our troubles is negative.

That's not always true. I've seen families who even the most untrained eye would label as dysfunctional. But within that family, mixed up as they are, one person—a child, a mother, a father—turned things around by opening up the conversation and talking about what had been troubling them for years.

When a family first comes for counseling, I point to the purple heart sitting on my table and say, "Since we only have an hour together, let's go directly to the heart of the matter." Then I say, "Tell me: What's troubling you?" Dewey was nine years old when parents brought him to counseling. He had difficulty sitting still, couldn't concentrate in school, and was bullying his classmates. His mother and father were concerned that he was dropping behind. I asked him to hold the heart and speak of all his troubles, and I asked his parents to listen without interrupting. Dewey talked about hating his teacher and thinking it wasn't fair that he had to come right home and do homework before he went outside. When he was through, Dewey passed the heart to his dad and said, "It's your turn." Dad told about his troubles as a child. As boy, he lived on a farm and had to milk cows right after school and then do his homework with never any time for loafing. When Dad was done, it was Mom's turn to share her troubles. Then our hour was up. The next week the family came back, and I said, "Let's get to the heart of the matter." Each person held the heart and talked about their troubles. This continued for five weeks. On the sixth session I asked, "How are things going?" They all answered, "Much better." Other than giving the parents a book to read and a few suggestions here and there, I hadn't performed any magic, yet their troubles were lighter.

All families have troubles. The problem is not that there are troubles, the problem is expecting that there shouldn't be. We need to share our troubles with each other. We need to let our children see that we too have troubles so they can know how we're working them out. When we share our disappointments, let downs, and blues with each other, we gain more strength and learn more ways of coping. That's because we understand ourselves best with the help of others. Talking about the heart of the matter, difficult though it may be, is surprisingly refreshing. Don't you agree that a purple talking-heart is a good investment for your table?

Hang a Suggestion Box

Margaret bought an antique suggestion box at an auction. She had no ulterior motive; she simply wanted it as a decorative piece. She arranged it on the coffee table next to the antique kaleidoscope and gum-ball dispenser. Eleven-year-old Libby spotted the box immediately and asked, "Do I get to make suggestions?" Before Margaret could answer, Libby was pulling out her notebook and writing down three recommendations. As soon as nine-year-old Nathan heard that Libby had made suggestions, he did the same. When Dad came home, they showed him the box and bugged him until he put in his three and persuaded Mom to do the same. Nathan wanted to read the suggestions right away, but Libby insisted they wait until fifteen-year-old Andrea got home so she could put in hers. When they finally read them, the suggestions ranged from the practical, "After dinner everyone puts their own dishes in the dishwasher," to the playful, "Make every Wednesday pizza night." The suggestion box was so much fun they now use it as a generator of ideas, a problem solver, and a conversation starter.

In a lively, interactive family, everyone contributes both elbow grease by doing household maintenance and ideas by making suggestions on family matters. If kids don't feel they have a say in how things are run, they will take every chance they can to make themselves scarce; for who wants to live with tyrants?

For some kids and adults, it's easier to express themselves on paper. Keep a daily logbook next to the telephone or a family journal open on the coffee table so that each of you can write messages, jot down ideas, voice complaints, or ask questions. You might initiate the process by writing a question of the week: What would you like to change about our family life? What would you like to do for fun that takes thirty minutes? What shall we cook for dinner next week? You may get one-sentence answers or a whole page. The length doesn't matter, it's the joy of contributing that you're teaching. Set aside time each week for reading and discussing the suggestions.

Family life is fun when you try new approaches. When you consider your partner's and children's suggestions, you're keeping children interested and active in their home life. Bob, a single father of three very active teenagers, uses the family log for keeping track of upcoming events, "Morgan's tennis match, Friday," "Rob wants the car for the prom in three weeks," and for making requests, "Help, I need one volunteer to go with me to the grocery store, one to clean out the garage, and one to rearrange the pantry." If you sprinkle your requests with a few riddles, advice, jokes, nonsense, and friendly gossip, you'll keep the troops curious and reading. If you offer incentives such as, "The first one who answers gets a coupon for a hamburger and shake," you'll keep the excitement going.

Be Willing to Be Wrong

To have healthy relationships with your loved ones, you have to be willing to admit when you are wrong. By admitting your flaws, your errors in judgment, your mistakes, your thoughtlessness, your mess-ups, the nasty little things you do, you're clearing the way to your loved one's heart. Take full credit for your inadequacies. Your partner and your children know you better than anyone else: they see who you are, they know your imperfections. When you own up to your mistakes, the fountain of compassion begins to flow. By admitting how you've goofed up, you gain a badge of honesty, and it allows them to be human too.

You probably know someone who won't admit when they're wrong. James is like that. He has a chip on his shoulder and gets defensive over the slightest things. When his wife, Molly, asks him, "Why are you yelling?" he's sarcastic, quick to snap back, and he points his finger at her, with "You're a good one to talk!" He has opinions about everything, including things he knows nothing about. He argues with his wife, his children, his friends, and strangers. He insists he is right and won't listen to other points of view. He's always defending himself. It probably won't surprise you that Molly and the kids don't talk to Dad much. They avoid emotional subjects, politics, and religion. They don't share their opinions for fear that Dad might get his tail feathers ruffled. Sadly, many families get stuck in this superficial manner of relating, avoiding each other and stagnating as a consequence.

People of character acknowledge their faults and their blunders. They're willing to learn from their little and big mistakes, see the error of their ways, and make changes. They admit, "I'm mistaken." They acknowledge, "I'm wrong." They know that no matter how mature or experienced they are, they and everyone else is still learning, stumbling, and finding their way.

Mistakes attest to the fact that you're actively living. If you're never wrong, either you're not taking any chances or you're browbeating your children and partner into agreeing with you. Insisting that you're always right is a sure sign of that you are stuck in the "inferiority well." The only way to gain strength and climb out of your complex is to accept responsibility for your behavior. Instead of blaming others, bad luck, your parents, or the moon, open to see what God is trying to reveal to you. Owning up to your flaws is an indication that you recognize your human condition and are ready to grow. Seeing yourself in the light of truth allows you to make changes.

As a parent or a spouse you don't have to know all the right answers. In fact, we gain the admiration of family members when we admit we don't know everything. As fourteen-year-old Jason said, "I respected my dad so much when he said he was wrong."

When you open to the possibility that you might be wrong, like confession, it's good for your soul.

Get over Grudges Quickly

A grudge is a long-standing resentment that carries with it a deep-seated feeling of spite, bitterness, and hostility. Grudges, like wet wool blankets, cover life with clouds of heaviness until you begin seeing everything as if a dark storm is looming on the horizon. When you look at life through the haze of grudges, you can't see clearly, you can't enjoy sunshine, you lose your joy. Grudges have a way of oozing ill will, infecting all relationships, both with family and friends. They make you suspicious and destroy all chances for love. If you've ever carried a grudge for even one day, you know how it saps your energy. Letting grudges fester destroys your peace of mind, guaranteeing incessant misery and suffering.

Grudges accumulate for more reasons then we can list here. Perhaps as a child you were not allowed to speak up or voice your preferences. Perhaps you wanted everything to be "nice" so you never made waves, showed you were upset, or appeared angry. Perhaps you've lived with someone who was so volatile that you had to walk on eggshells to avoid raging explosions. Perhaps you're afraid of loving.

Whatever the reasons for your grudges, their causes don't matter as much as what you do with them. Mulling them over for weeks, months, or years is not conducive to fulfilling relationships. Getting over them, repairing the wounds, and moving on, is.

Here are some tips to get you over grudges:

1. List on a sheet of paper every grudge and resentment that pops into your head. Don't censor.

2. Go back over the list and put an "S" by the grudges that are more than one month old. These are slush-fund grudges, which require direct intervention. Put a star by all the others. (These are recent resentments that can be easily corrected.)

3. Make an appointment with an impartial person—a minister, a counselor, a trusted confidante, a mentor, a wise person.

4. Tell the person about each slush-fund grudge and what purpose it has served.

5. Go home, read over your grudges one by one, and say good-bye to the pain and suffering they have caused you. For example, say out loud, "I let go of this grudge toward my mother; it's not serving me any longer."

6. Starred grudges that are less than a month old should be handled in another way, which you can read about in the next essay, Be Willing to Make Waves.

A word of caution about slush-fund grudges: It is not necessary to convey, confront, blast, or otherwise communicate your slush-fund grudges to your family. When you've been carrying grudges for years, they might not even remember what you're talking about. What is important is that you identify your grudges for yourself, communicate them to a trusted confidante, then consciously choose to let them go.

Be Willing to Make Waves

Resentments develop when you don't express yourself as completely or as directly as you need too. Biting your tongue at times is beneficial, but not if it gives birth to resentment. Often it's actually better for your relationships if instead of keeping quiet, you speak up. In other words, in order to keep your relationships thriving, sometimes you must be willing to make waves.

Resentments are caused by doing things you don't want to do and then behaving like a martyr. Nothing destroys relationships quicker than towers of resentments and mountains of hidden anger. If you live in a family, you'll get angry. Just as it's human to get thirsty, so is it human to get angry. Just as it's necessary to take a drink of water to quench your thirst, it's necessary to communicate your frustrations to avoid them piling up. Your family will be closer when you recognize your anger, express your anger appropriately, and allow them to do the same. When you accept that making waves is healthy, you won't have to walk on eggshells around each other.

Thirteen-year-old Sydney was angry at her father and adamantly told him what she was thinking, "Just because Lily has spiked hair doesn't mean she's not a good friend. You don't even know her." Jake, not interested in seeing his daughter's point of view, warned her, "Keep that up and you'll be grounded." In fact, he enforced the "don't make waves" policy whenever his children expressed any anger or disagreed with him. He thought it was disrespectful for children to disagree or be angry with their parents. It was okay if his children expressed anger at some injustice in the outside world, but expressing disagreement toward him was not allowed. Those disagreements had to be kept under wraps.

A "don't make waves" policy has lasting negative effects on family relationships. Hiding your thoughts and keeping your feelings in check can put a strained distance between you. Now, rather than expressing herself directly, Sydney hides her thoughts, disguises her opinions, and takes her frustrations out in other, less healthy, ways. And because she has to put her energy into pretending, a distance has grown between her and her father. Years from now when Jake wonders why his children don't talk to him about important things in their lives, when he wonders why there is tension in the air when they are together, it just may be because his children stopped sharing long ago.

Do you have a few waves that you need to make? Is there something you need to complain about but have avoided? What is it? As you recognize your anger, you'll understand it's purpose and won't be thrown for such a loop when your child or spouse is angry. You'll understand that anger is a signal and that you need to listen to what the other person is saying so that together you can make the necessary adjustments. Making waves, after all, is really a communication process of give and take.

Timing is important when it comes to delivering the message. The closer to the event that you can communicate your disgruntlement the more effective you will be. If you have any new resentments starting to pile up, ask yourself, "What is this about?" and let the other person know what you're thinking. Be specific about the changes you're asking them to make. Be gracious and let them do the same with you.

Brainstorm for Solutions

Today's families face big challenges, particularly families with young children and teens and where both parents work outside the home or where a single parent is struggling to do it all. There's the stress of not enough time, not enough money, not enough rest, too many activities, too much pressure, and too much work. Families are fragmented as never before. Our ancestors' lives weren't any easier; in many ways they were harder. However, there was more of a sense of community because they spent more time together. Girls spent more time with their mothers and boys with their fathers. In order for the family to survive, literally, they had to work together.

Modern families are going in different directions, spending more time out of the home than in it. Young children in day care often spend more of their waking hours with sitters and teachers than with their own parents. Teens' lives are full with school, extracurricular activities, and socializing. Parents, feeling swamped with all their obligations, dream of unpressured family time.

Modern family life requires collaborative effort. You have to pull together and brainstorm for solutions. When you pitch in to address whatever problem you're facing, you can accomplish many things. You'll be surprised at the solutions you can come up with when you combine your brain power.

The Moores have a large family—two parents, three children, three foster children, two dogs, a dozen or more rabbits, seven homing pigeons, and a tropical fish aquarium. On the bulletin board in the kitchen is an oversized calendar where everyone keeps track of their appointments. Alongside it is an erasable sign-out board where family members post their comings and goings. Next to that, is the chalk board where the weekly and monthly chores are posted. "To keep our family running smoothly," Ellen told me, "we need operating procedures." They establish, modify, change, amend, and smooth out the kinks every other Monday night at a family council meeting. Twice a month they address problems, share mutual concerns, talk about their individual dreams, and organize family events such as pigeon races. As needed, they reinvent operating procedures, design action plans, and support each other. "To succeed we have to pull together," said Marvin. "We hold council because the more brain power the better." They take turns running the meetings; "We have operating procedures for family council too," laughed fourteen-year-old Joey.

From rotating the chores to what new fish to buy to the television programs allowed, they discuss the questions in a spirit of fair play. The head of the council is responsible for the agenda and making sure that everyone is heard; when necessary he or she might make the final decision. Everything is open for negotiation—from why the teenagers can stay out later to why Mom did Katy's chores last week to requests for extra spending money. In so doing, the kids are learning problem solving. If the boys have been fighting over the dirt bikes, they have to come up with a solution. The meetings are heated and lively because they don't always see eye to eye, but as they work through their struggles, they are becoming closer as a family.

Establish Sensible Guidelines

As head of your household, you know that your family needs structure. You've probably heard experts talk about setting limits, creating boundaries, and making rules. You know it's important, yet you've probably asked yourself, "How do I know what rules are appropriate, what is reasonable, what works best?" You may not want your guidelines to be like the ones you grew up with, but the ones the neighbors use don't seem appropriate for your family either. From the terrible twos through the incredible teens, you'll need to establish sensible guidelines to keep you happily enjoying all phases of your children's development. It's a big undertaking, and there are no quick solutions. It's a daily adventure of trying new ideas, fine tuning, and going forward.

The guidelines that are the most suitable to family life are those that create confidence, reduce fears, and make each member comfortable. Most of us have to keep practicing to get good at something. A few folks are good at what they do from the start, but most people aren't. That's why sensible guidelines incorporate a learning curve, allowing each member to learn about themselves and each other. Sensible guidelines also allow for expression of feelings and exploration of ideas, and they take into consideration stressful situations such as illness, divorce, accidents, separation from friends, or just a plain old bad day.

When establishing guidelines for your family, make sure that you allow each other to speak out about feelings while limiting undesirable behavior. You want guidelines that build character and self-esteem, not tear down self-respect.

Sensible guidelines are built on these principles:

1. Always assume the best about each other.
2. Update your rules as needed. Bending serves a purpose too.
3. Every family member has the right to participate fully and, whenever possible, be given a choice in the matters that affect him or her.
4. Treat each other kindly—no put downs allowed.
5. The best balance is more rewards, less criticism.
6. Give latitude for learners and for stressful situations.
7. Lighten up and promote a sense of humor about family matters.

Guidelines are a safety feature that gives children a predictable base and a consistency they can count on. "My husband and I believed it was our responsibility to give our children the tools they needed to deal with whatever life had in store for them," notes Anna. "As society needs structure and rules to exist and progress, so do our children." Guidelines are meant to help families live harmoniously. That doesn't mean that you can't disagree, but that when you do, you know that in the process everyone is actively included.

Keep Rules Flexible

After one month of college, my daughter Amanda told me that she could really see the difference between her classmates who had experienced personal freedom before going away to school and the kids who hadn't had much control over their lives. She said that students discuss the differences and agreed among themselves that the kids who partied the hardest were the ones who had been the most controlled by their parents. It was as if they'd never stayed up late, never had a say over their lives, and were trying to a make up for lost time. They were going wild with their new freedoms and couldn't settle down.

Families do need standards and parents need to enforce guidelines with sensitivity to the needs of their children at the time. But you need to keep things in perspective. It doesn't harm anyone if you let your five-year-old skip her bath occasionally. It's okay if your eight-year-old can't keep his room organized. Children's needs change, and parents need to be able to respond appropriately to the needs of each stage of development. Every family needs principles of behavior, guidelines for what is acceptable and what isn't. What you don't need is a rigid set of laws that turn you into a police officer.

Negotiating household rules and reviewing family guidelines on an individual basis and personal merit leads to cooperation. You'll have less policing to do and less enforcing. It's human nature that when you give your children a say in coming up with the expectations, they're invested in seeing that they work. Rules aren't meant to constrict us. Rules should help us, not impede us.

Take curfews, for example. Instead of setting a hard-and-fast curfew for each and every occasion, if you give your teenager the opportunity to state the time that would be appropriate to come home after the dance, she won't feel the need to rebel. One study found that kids who had to argue and fight for later curfews, or had an absolute curfew, seem to stay out later than kids whose curfews were flexible depending on the event and the mood. If your fifteen-year-old is over at a friend's house and having fun, wanting to stay later, but he knows if he calls you, you'll pitch a fit, he might postpone the confrontation and not call. But if he knows that you will consider his request, he'll be more likely to call and let you know what's up.

It's the same with bedtime schedules. Children's need for sleep varies almost week to week. Letting your child learn about how much sleep they need by giving your permission to stay up later when they ask, will save you years of wear and tear. Soon, instead of begging for another drink of water or making endless trips to the bathroom, they'll simply go to bed when they're sleepy.

Face the Enemy

We cannot talk about the wonderful ways to be a family without facing the enemy: The number one killer of families is alcohol and substance abuse. It has destroyed more children than lack of parenting skills. It has ruined more marriages than divorce. It has torn apart more families than any other factor. Alcoholism and substance abuse ravages self-confidence, makes intimacy impossible, and stunts the soul's growth. It's an emotional, physical, and spiritual affliction that hurts every family member. If you grew up in an alcoholic home, you were infected; if you're presently living with a drinking alcoholic or drug abuser, you're in danger.

Substance abuse will devastate your family. The majority of child abuse is alcohol and drug related. Allowing your children to grow up with a drinking alcoholic or drug addict will more than likely leave your children emotionally crippled. Their chances of becoming an alcoholic or marrying one is increased. They'll suffer from a vast array of difficulties ranging from depression to shame to compulsive overachieving. Children who can't trust their parents to protect them from this destroyer of goodness grow up having difficulties trusting themselves and others.

Alcoholism and drug addiction are your enemy. If you grew up in an alcoholic home, you need to educate yourself about its affects. If you're married to an alcoholic, you absolutely must behave responsibly and face it. Alcoholism and drug addiction are treatable afflictions, but when you avoid confronting your opponent, you have no chance of victory; you and your family will be lost in the clutches of denial. To get free from its grip you must take a firm stand. Pretending that alcohol is not a problem when you suspect it might be, looking the other way when your husband is high, takes a lasting toll on you and your children. It robs you of your joy, it saps your energy. Stand firm, educate yourself, and be courageous.

If your spouse is abusing alcohol or drugs, you have a moral obligation on behalf of your precious children to take action. Begin by educating yourself about substance abuse. In cities all across our country, thousands and thousands of courageous families have received help from Alanon, Alcoholics Anonymous, and Adult Children of Alcoholics. Look in the telephone book for their numbers, and call them immediately. Don't wait! Your family is in danger. Contact a family counselor who is trained in this area, and make an appointment.

Memorize the following and either write a letter to your spouse or say it directly: "I know that you're not drinking (or using drugs) for fun. I hope you'll get help. I know there is nothing I can do if you won't. It's your decision. I am getting help for myself and our children." Then stand firm for the sake of your family. Enlist friends and family for assistance in staying on course. Stand firm and save your children; it will be worth it.

Enforce What Needs to Be Enforced

I'm from the relationship school of parenting, which means I place my emphasis on creating a loving relationship between parents and children. To me, the most important aspect of family life is the quality of the relationship between you and other family members. I advocate negotiation on most family matters. But once in a while, it's necessary to borrow from the authoritarian school and put your foot down.

William, the father of five grown children and grandfather of seven told me, "My children were given the freedom to form their own ideas, to question, and to sometimes change particular family rules, but they also were expected to comply with our final decision on those we deemed essential. They were told when they had their own family, then this responsibility would fall to them." Kathleen, the mother of two spirited boys, ages five and seven said, "I'm easy, and I don't mind being coaxed or talked into something, but I don't allow biting, hitting, whining, or breaking the law."

Children feel more secure when they know the borders of acceptable conduct. They need clear definitions of what's permissible in your family and what isn't. For example, angry feelings are permissible, but not angry acts. Five-year-old Cody slammed the door and kicked the cat. His mom said, "You're mad inside? What's up?" Cody answered, "You didn't fix my bike!" Mom answered, "You're right. I said I'd fix it, and I will this afternoon. When you're mad at me, come tell me, but don't be mean to the cat."

Clear limits should clarify what's not acceptable and what is in a strong way: "Hit the boxing bag, not your brothers." "Biting is not allowed." You want your child to know that you mean business on these matters. Tell your children what you expect: "You can be mad at your sister, but no hurting allowed." "No walking to the store after dark." "The chair is for sitting, not jumping."

Sometimes the situation is not as clear, or it catches you off guard, and you're ill prepared. When that happens, it's best to take the time to think it through before you take a stand. Your children know when you're waffling, and waffling leads to incessant arguing and a battle of wills.

Limit setting should convey your authority. Don't insult your children or shame them into complying. If you know what behavior you expect and why, if you're sure of yourself before you act, if you avoid put downs and name calling, your children will usually comply. Don't be argumentative or belittle your child in any way. And don't be verbose—a little common sense can go a long way in figuring out what needs to be enforced, but whatever you do, please don't talk in chapters.

Ignore the Small Stuff

We've all been tempted to say, "If you think you've got problems, you should hear mine." That must have been what Kay, the mother of five kids ages six to sixteen, was thinking the day she told me this story: "Our neighbor Kent called me at work yesterday afternoon and wondered whether my kids wanted to raise a 4-H lamb this year. Elise said no, but Megan and Matt said yes. Kent had lambs that they could buy, so he hauled them down with his kids and their lambs to do the official weigh-in for the summer. I took the mail to the post office and when I got back, Kent and Matt arrived with the lambs. We now have a ewe and little twin lambs in our back field, along with Nicole's horse and our calf.

"Then Elise got all upset because she decided that lambs looked fun after all. So I made arrangements to get one for her, and I'm taking it down to town at 7:30 tomorrow morning to be weighed in! In the middle of all that, a neighbor called to say that three of our heifers and a calf had gotten loose and were headed for the main road! So I got Matt and Jared to go with me, and we drove the cows through town in the rain, back to the field. When we got there, the other ones were getting out. I got in the truck and asked Kent if he could bring his trailer and help us haul the cattle to the ranch. It was raining and extremely muddy, but we finally got them loaded and back at the ranch by 9:00 p.m.! Then I fed everyone, gave the baby a bath, and put him to bed.

"Barking dogs woke me up about 1:30 a.m., and I could hear deep animal breathing outside my window. I thought Nicole's horse had gotten out, so I put on my robe and tennis shoes, and went outside. All of a sudden, two huge bulls raced right by me and crossed the highway! Was I scared! I worried about someone running into them and being killed! I called the sheriff's office, but the deputies, who are good friends of ours, were asleep. The dispatcher said, 'There sure are a lot of animals out lately! We just had several cows in our yard a couple of days ago!' Guess whose cattle those probably were? Nicole and I got in our truck and drove down the street to see if the bulls were still on the highway. Remember, this is about 2:00 a.m. We couldn't find them, so I was hoping that they had taken off down a side road. We went back to bed, but I kept my window open all night half listening for them. I had told my son's teacher that I couldn't help with the Dutch oven cookout tonight, and I'm so glad I did! I think I'm going to get better and better at saying no! Heck, just to keep up with all our 'normal' stuff is a full-time job!"

Moral: If it isn't cattle loose in the back yard, it's sure to be something else, so you might as well ignore the small stuff and have a good chuckle.

Curb Harsh Words

How many times have you said something you didn't mean? Lashed out? Spoken without thinking about the impact of your words?

My friend Chloe was sitting on a park bench when a mother and her four-year-old son sat down beside her. The boy, wiggling and smiling, was cute as a button. Chloe asked him, "What's your name?" "Sam," he answered. His mother piped in with, "But we call him Brat." Startled by such an announcement, Chloe said, "What a shame!" The mother, trying to smooth it over, said, "Oh, we're just teasing." Chloe wisely responded, "Oh, but he won't know that."

Words can hurt or heal, tear down or inspire—so be careful what you say. Words can slaughter self-confidence, ravish self-esteem, and tear your relationships to shreds. In some cases what you say can cause irrevocable harm, shaking your loved one to the core.

In fits of anger it's best to keep quiet and watch your tongue. When you're mad and you want to get even, be aware that nasty remarks will hurt, possibly devastating your loved ones. If you're honest, isn't that the reason you're thinking of saying them? When you do try to get even, you end up feeling worse and are trapped into justifying your obnoxious words by pleading, "Oh, I didn't mean it." Saying the first cruel thing that pops into your mind shows that you've lost control of yourself. Getting even with each other, playing tit-for-tat, poisons your relationship with a cloud of impending doom.

If you're upset and tempted to say something cruel, it's best to take a break by saying: "Let's talk later when we've both had a chance to calm down" or "I'm feeling upset by what you said and I need a chance to think it over." Then you can express your feelings in a more constructive manner. Instead of saying, "I'm sick of your sourpuss face," try saying "It's not a good day for you." Statements of understanding bear sympathy and love.

Avoid words that criticize or condemn. Don't compare your children to each other. Remember, brisk, sharp questions like, "Why did you do that?" or "How many times do I have to tell you?" convey harshness and break your loved one's spirit. Avoid threats, "If you don't knock it off, I'll give you something to cry about," and accusations, "You always do that." Balance any criticism with generous appreciation, "I appreciate your sweeping the steps, but I'm disappointed that you didn't complete the task we agreed you'd do this afternoon."

Watch out for the labels you place on each other. Labels limit our potential. They make us treat our children and partners in a prescribed way, i.e., colicky, temperamental, hyper, slow learner, big shot, shrimp, prissy, stubborn. Also, behave yourself in public. Don't criticize your children or spouse in front of others. If you talk badly about them, it makes you look ridiculous.

One of the things that you don't want to fail at is the relationship with your family. Curbing harsh words and stating your requirements without adding insults will go alone way to guaranteeing success. Please don't say something that can never be forgotten.

Negotiate at the Peace Table

There's a tremendous exhilaration when families discover that they can vent their grievances and negotiate their solutions without hurting each other. The politics of peace begin with agreeing to air your grievances gently and to hear the other's point of view. It's a preventative movement that goes a long way to solidifying your relationships. If you adults can do it, your kids will learn how too.

Marleena, who was always insisting that her family keep their home clean and neat according to "my standards," was stopped in her tracks one day when asked by her husband and ten-year-old daughter, "Why do you think your way is the best way for us to live?" "At first I was defensive and argumentative," she confessed, "but after sitting on a park bench thinking about what they'd said, I had to agree that they had a point. I was fanatical about the house and knew I could benefit by a more relaxed approach. Over the next couple of nights we negotiated a workable arrangement. The kitchen, front hall, and bathroom would be kept up to my standards, and I would relax about the other family areas. Since I was willing to see their point of view and compromise, they were more willing to cooperate."

Eight-year-old Adam and nine-year-old Joel were locked in a battle of sibling rivalry. Maggie knew it was natural for brothers to fight, argue, and insult each other—she even told them so. Usually she was able to let them resolve it without getting involved, but this afternoon their fighting seemed to be getting out of hand; at the very least it was getting on her nerves. She took them by the hands and said, "We're going to talk this over at the peace table." Sitting them at the kitchen table, she poured juice, and prepared cheese and crackers while telling them that their fighting and name calling was causing unhappiness. "I expect this quarrel to be settled without insults. I want to know what's bothering you." Each told their side without interruptions, and each rebutted until they had nothing more to say. "Now what are the solutions?" she asked. "Which one can you live with?" After they had come up with a solution, Maggie said, "Okay, we'll meet back at the peace table tomorrow to see how peace is going."

Would it work for you to designate a neutral spot in your house as the peace table, the peace bench, or the peace corner? Negotiating begins with airing grievances gently and listening without defending yourself. Complaints, little annoyances, and disagreements can be successfully negotiated. Asking to go to the peace bench means you're ready to air grievances gently and negotiate livable solutions. It means being willing to stop defending yourself and attacking each other—that you are ready to compromise and follow up. Even when your kids can't come up with a peaceful solution right away, talking at the peace table eases tensions—and eventually they'll get the idea.

Willingly Patch Things Up

Apologizing has been grossly overlooked as one of the best ways for healing old and new wounds so that you can fully partake in the smorgasbord of wonderful adventures that go with being a family member. Apologizing keeps the cobwebs of complaints from taking hold, keeps haunting resentments from strangling the affection between you. When you apologize, you feel better. Apologizing lets you walk tall because you've taken the high road: "I'm sorry, I wasn't listening." "I'm sorry for being so cranky." "I was wrong for borrowing your jacket without asking." "I was wrong for snooping in your room." "You're right! I messed up."

An apology made after careful reflection and an inner search is an elixir for the glitches in your relationship. It prevents loyalty from turning sour, puts an end to grievances, and unlocks the gates to forgiveness. It opens the way for a fresh start by restoring dignity to each of you.

As a partner to your mate and a parent to your children, you will make mistakes—too much criticism here; not enough attention there. Recognizing when you've blown it, apologizing for your actions, and changing your behavior clears the way for affability, while hiding your blunders and slipups leads to dead-end conversations and a widening gulf between you. With a sincere apology, you can avoid the blame game: "He made me do it." "It's her fault." "You're too sensitive; it's no big deal." No need to point the finger when you're willing to admit the error of your ways.

When six-year-old Craig saw the neighbor boy carrying his bear skin rug away, he questioned his mom, "What's Zack doing with my rug?" "You didn't want it," Jane explained, "so I sold it at the garage sale." "But it's *my* rug," Craig said. Perturbed by the fuss he was making Jane pointed out, "But it's been crumpled up in the back of your closet for months. Besides you'll get the money." Later, Jane, realizing her mistake, apologized to Craig for selling his property and for getting upset when he objected. Since she had felt she had the right to clean out his closet without asking, she also apologized for being disrespectful.

If you find it difficult to say "I'm sorry" in person, begin by writing apology notes. Sandra wrote to her fifteen-year-old son, Jeremy, "I am wrong for listening into your telephone conversation. I won't do it again. Please give me another chance to prove that I am trustworthy." Two months later Jeremy wrote a note to his mother using the same format, "I am wrong for calling you names. Please give me another chance to prove that I am trustworthy." Sandra told her parenting group that apology notes have given them both the courage to apologize face to face.

Apologizing shows your character, reflects your self-esteem, and frees you from the past. When you own up to the hurt you've caused, you won't be plagued by guilt. Admitting your flaws—yes, we all have them—is a measure of personal integrity.

Talk About What Truly Matters

Emotional connectedness is the Superglue that keeps a family close, the foundation for meaningful, fulfilling relationships. We all yearn to be intimately connected—to know each other deeply. During our lifespan, the person who fulfills our need for closeness changes. A new baby bonds to his parents in order to develop. A teenager wants connection and approval while venturing out and becoming autonomous. As adults, our need for closeness with our parents diminishes as we turn to our chosen partner for physical and emotional intimacy. Married couples turn to each other for acceptance, affection, attention, and affirmation. Single parents turn to adult friendships for warmth and understanding.

To stay emotionally healthy, it's imperative that you have your emotional needs met. But it isn't appropriate for you to expect your children to fulfill your longings. Emotionally healthy parents depend on each other and adult friends for comfort and support. They know they need to be "filled up" so that they can give their children the abundant support, care, compassion, and understanding they need.

One way of achieving emotional connectedness is through talking about what truly matters. By sharing your dreams, hopes, fears, and aspirations, you become intimate. Opening your heart and exposing your secrets strengthens your capacity to love.

Intimacy is the satisfying experience of sharing your innermost being; it can be seen to mean in-to-me-see. Whether you're single or married, it takes effort. If your married, you have to get in the habit of intimacy. During twenty years of marriage instead of getting closer, Michael and Sarah grew apart. Instead of talking about his restlessness and his dream to travel the world on a sail boat, Michael talked about sports and threw himself into his work. Instead of sharing her insecurities and her dream of graduating from college, Sarah kept busy with friends, children, and her part-time job. When the last child graduated from high school, Michael and Sarah had to work hard to get reacquainted.

If you're not married, when you confide in friends, you reap the rewards of having more emotional energy. Your family benefits too. If you depend solely on your children, they feel smothered and are unnecessarily crippled by the added emotional pressure. When your children see that you're able to meet your own emotional needs, they learn about healthy relationships and are able to maintain a balanced level of closeness.

Make time in your weekly schedule to talk with your partner, if you have one, or if you don't, a friend. Close out distractions, empty your mind of your to-do list, and talk about what truly matters. Share your hopes, dreams, and secret wishes. Look at your life and ask yourself what's missing. Is there anything you'd like to do differently? Another direction you'd like to pursue? Have the courage to talk about the real dilemma's your family is facing. Patricia, widowed at thirty-seven and mother of two sons, belongs to a support group where she can talk about her grief, her agony of having to go back to work, and her fears of raising her sons on her own. Talking about what truly matters rejuvenates your soul, giving you courage to carry on.

Put Your Accent on Inner Beauty

Are you cheerful? Are you open to life or have you closed for fear of further pain? Are you willing to risk being called a fool to stand for what is true? Do you accept failure and get up and try again? Are you willing to risk following your heart to find your dreams?

Well-adjusted parents with happy children emphasize those qualities that sustain them through the hard times. It isn't things that make us happy, it isn't glamour or good looks, it's heart connections. It's developing yourself—knowing what you think, feel, and value. It's tapping into invisible sources of comfort. It's knowing what makes your heart sing.

In today's consumer society, many families are trapped by the belief that possessions, appearances, and achievements make us happy. Billboards proclaim that the keys to happiness are muscles, skinny bodies, fast cars, fake fingernails, and lots of cash. Advertisers want us to believe that if we buy the right sneakers, the right jeans, and the right beer, we'll have it made. How are these messages influencing you and your family? Celebrities, movie stars, and basketball players have become today's role models. Who are your children's heroes? Who do you admire? Many people complain that we're being brainwashed by the media while participating in it. What magazines do you read?

When you think about human needs, it's really quite simple. Families need a roof over their heads, food, meaningful work, medical care, friendship, honesty, and compassion. Children need good guidance.

Talk to your children about inner beauty and qualities of the heart. Tell them that lasting beauty shines from within, it rises from the soul. Talk about the people who demonstrate character by doing the right thing. Acknowledge your child for saying no to something he knew he shouldn't do. Choose a motto for the week and paste it on the refrigerator. Keep copies of "The Ugly Duckling" and "The Emperor's New Clothes" for handy reference. The messages are appropriate reminders for all ages. Stock your house with inspiring movies such as *Chariots of Fire*, *Phenomenon*, and *Forrest Gump*.

Read "Cinderella" aloud. It teaches the value of modesty, cheerfulness, hard work, and kindness. Cinderella had nothing, but even after her father had died, her outlook was positive, while her stepsisters had everything and were miserable. They plotted, schemed, lied, and cheated, which made them ugly. Cinderella, on the other hand, wore rags, treated the smallest creatures kindly, and remained lighthearted. She trusted the unseen forces guiding her life and was sent a miracle. Isn't that the inner beauty you want your child to emulate?

As a wise person once said, "Values are not taught, they're caught." Values are not imparted through speeches, lectures, or commandments, but rather absorbed by identifying with the people we love and respect.

Always Make the Highest Choice

If you're an adult, you have a sacred covenant to the wonderful family of human beings—the family to which we all belong—to make the highest choice and to ceaselessly do the right thing. It's a sacred obligation that comes with being human.

In order to make the highest choice and do the right thing, it's imperative that you understand the dynamic of ambivalence. Ambivalence is defined as the coexistence of opposing attitudes or feelings, such as love and hate, toward a person, an object, or an idea.

Ambivalence is part of our inner makeup—meaning we all can feel contrasting feelings at the same time. For example, you can like your mother one minute and hate her the next. You can adore your husband yet get so mad at him that you wonder why you married him in the first place. You can cherish your baby with all your heart, yet in a moment of frustration come very close to shaking her.

Ambivalence is a fact of life. It resides in you and in your children. You can feel two ways about the people you love. You can love them and dislike them. You can feel admiration for your sister's success and jealous that you haven't made it yet. You can be devoted to your friend and secretly hold hostility.

If you aren't aware of these double sets of feelings, you're likely to be mixed up, messed up, confused, and not sure what to do when you and your mom, or you and your husband don't see eye to eye. By recognizing ambivalent feelings, instead of building a case against them, you're better prepared to make the highest choice and do the right thing. You have free will to act.

People who aren't comfortable with their own ambivalent feelings get intrigued by them. It's like this: If I were to point and tell you, "Don't look over there," you'd be really tempted; in fact you might become obsessed. Likewise if I say, "don't be mad," you might not be able to get over it. But if I said it's okay to look and it's okay to feel, you are free to choose how long to look and what action to take.

In confusing situations, becoming aware of your ambivalence helps you choose the right thing. Jason was thinking about quitting the team. His dad said, "You feel two ways about your coach—you like him and you dislike him. You want to quit the team because you don't like the way the coach yells, but you want to stay on the team because you like your teammates and the coach lets you pitch." After Jason said all that he had to say, his dad asked, "What do you think is the right thing to do?" Jason said, "Stay on the team"; and that's exactly what he did.

When you're confused and not sure what to do, ask yourself, "What is my highest choice?" Get in the habit of asking, "In this situation, what is the right thing to do?" Your immediate family, your extended family, and your innocent children and pets are counting on you to make the highest choice and do the right thing.

Use the Creative Approach

Have you ever noticed that there are families who seem to have it all because they have a zest for living? When you're with them life is rich with endless possibilities. They aren't trying to keep up with the neighbors; instead they're absorbed in their own pursuits. They're not competing with one another; rather they are enjoying being together. They don't waste time with negative thinking, because they have so much they want to explore and accomplish; they want to make a contribution, taste all of life, and live with gusto. They're curious, cheerful, resourceful, and open minded. They take charge of their own lives and work hard to achieve personal goals.

A creative family is rich with possibilities and full of surprises. You achieve your potential by throwing away the "shoulds," "musts," and "have tos" in favor of "I choose." By designing a home life that suits your family, rather than doing it because "it seems to work for the neighbors," you'll be more effective in raising children who can think for themselves, trust in themselves, and have personal power.

When ten-year-old Charlie asked his dad, "Should I play the trumpet or saxophone?" Dad answered, "What do you think you'd like?" Then he helped Charlie investigate both instruments. When Erica asked her mom, "What should I wear to the party?" Fran wisely answered, "Why don't you talk to your friends to see what others suggest and then choose what you like best?"

Children gain confidence when given the opportunity to decide for themselves. Instead of demanding, "Do as you're told," it's empowering to send the message "You can decide what's right." By offering choices and allowing your children to make their own decisions, you're teaching them to trust their ability to solve problems rather than following others. For his eleventh birthday Josh was given a choice: "Would you like to play miniature golf or play games at the arcade?" "Neither," he said, "I'd rather go moonlight bowling."

Joilee asked her mom, "Can I get my belly button pierced? Everybody's doing it!" Instead of freaking out and saying, "If everyone jumped off a bridge, would you?" Maggie used the creative approach and said, "Think about all the pros and cons before you decide." She helped Joilee sort out all consequences and said, "Now, you can determine if it's right for you."

The creative approach encourages your child to please herself rather than others, which is good in the long run because if she knows what she likes and can state her opinions and preferences, she'll be sure of herself and be able to speak her own mind. Then she won't need to follow the crowd.

Every family has different needs; do what is appropriate for your family. If your mother-in-law criticizes your child-rearing practices, and you feel the need to explain, say, "This way is working best right now" or "We've decide to use the creative approach."

Cut Back on Spending

With two boys ages nine and eleven, Clark, a physical therapist, and Elena, a retail clerk, know that they have to practice inventive money management in order to cover all their financial bases. The kids are in a perpetual state of need, from new shoes for baseball, basketball, and track, to school supplies, new jeans, and the latest fads. From unexpected expenses due to mounds of wishes and wants, the family has learned the value of BWB—Budget, Wait, and Bargain.

Overspending can easily become an annoying habit that drags families down. Promoting financial well-being through budgeting, waiting for what it is that you really want, and hunting for bargains, is a better way to show your love than by putting your family in debt. (By the way, financial experts agree that paying off debt is a must for families living on a budget.) It's a vicious cycle: buying more than you need, going in debt, worrying about how to pay it off. If you always have financial pressures in the back of your mind, you can barely think of anything else. Out-of-whack money matters quickly spin into quarreling, overshadowing your enjoyment of each other.

How you choose to use your money can either add to your family life or detract from it. If you're in debt, you're probably worrying. If you're trying to keep up with the neighbors you're probably under too much pressure.

Remember: the way you and your spouse treat one another while taking financially inventory is more important than the figures on the paper. Some folks swear that if you can behave lovingly toward one another while making a budget, your marriage is secure. What are your family's financial goals? How much money do you make each month? How do you want to divide it? What is the happiest way to use it? When you pay off your debt, you can rejoice as you share in the mutual accomplishment.

Holding off, postponing, waiting to buy until it goes on sale, shopping at thrift stores, and looking for bargains is good family business—especially when you focus on the rewards of being a financially responsible person. In your best upbeat manner, tell your kids, "We're practicing financial fitness." Scolding, lecturing, or using "waiting to buy" as a punishment will make your children feel deprived; but emphasizing your admiration for their willingness to postpone or choose a bargain increases their capacity to deal with money slowdowns. When you let your children know how their thriftiness is contributing to the family's financial goals, they'll feel appreciated and valued.

After several years of intentional economizing, the Blaines were able to build up a nest egg so that Cindy could quit work and stay at home with the two kids. The Jamisons were able to save for their first family summer vacation. You and your children might participate with other family members or with another family in a "Moratorium on Spending:" Cut out all unnecessary expenditures for one or two weeks. Have each person keep a chart of what they wanted to spend and what they actually did spend. At the end of the day talk about how each person is doing. At the end of the moratorium compare notes with the other families participating in the project. How does it feel to cut back? Did it make a difference? Was your life worse or better? What are you learning about money and family life? One parent told me that she's learning that "Having enough is better for families than having it all."

Teach Social Graces and Good Sportsmanship

Social graces and good sportsmanship are little niceties, the frosting on our ordinary lives. Like candles on the cake, "Please" and "Thank you" add a glow to everyday encounters. Being a good sport, whether you win or lose the game, leaves a positive impression. It elevates your stance from participant to champion. Without the gestures of sportsmanship and good manners, daily interactions quickly turn sour.

I once had a client who grew up in the most horrific family. Her mother propped tiny mirrors in front of the children's plates and forced them to watch themselves as they ate. If they didn't use correct manners, chew silently, and take bite-size portions, they were hit with a belt that their parents kept prominently displayed at the table. Teaching manners and courtesy by threatening and brute force is not only cruel, it's crazy. You can probably train your children by threatening, badgering, berating, shaming, and belittling, but it won't do much for your relationship. You won't be a hero in their eyes.

When I talk about social graces, I'm not talking about super politeness and perfect table manners. Excited, energetic children talk with their mouths full and put their elbows on the table. When I talk about the social graces, I'm talking about how we treat each other. Being respectful and considerate to our neighbors, teachers, and all the other folks we interact with outside our homes melts antagonism and makes you—and the other person—feel good. It's enjoyable to be neighborly. That's why you do it. It has an additional benefit as well— saying "Thank you" to the teacher, the mailman, the paper boy, and the grocery-store checker inspires them toward kindness and thus makes the world a better place for us all to be in.

You don't have to send your kids to finishing to school to reach this goal; you achieve it by using *your* manners. Social graces are not difficult to teach if motivated by love. Love, after all, is the only source of lasting niceties.

Good sportsmanship is playing hard and obeying the rules. It's team spirit and treating teammates, opponents, and fans with courtesy. Playing fair is showing your enthusiasm for winning and behaving with dignity when losing. Good sportsmanship is the honorable way to go; it leaves a legacy of self-respect. Talk about what it means to be a good sport with your children, and practice it when you're playing games with them. Name your sports heroes, and describe how they demonstrate good sportsmanship. Show how they've benefitted from playing hard and fairly. Talk about the ones who've behaved badly and what that says about their character.

Remember: you advance sportsmanship by practicing what you're preaching. Leave the coaching to the coaches; don't grumble, mumble, swear, or complain. Always conduct yourself at games with honor and decorum. After all, good manners and sportsmanship are definitely cousins—ones we would all do well to know intimately.

Liven Up Your Routine

Nothing livens up your routine faster than doing a little favor for a family member: serving breakfast in bed, picking up dinner from the deli, changing the bed, giving a back rub, placing chocolate kisses on your honey's pillow, sending an unexpected treat hidden in a coat pocket, or giving a tiny present to your mom or dad "just because." Little wordless messages, as simple as bringing your sweet ones a drink of juice, don't take any time at all, but add so much sparkle to the moment that you'll wonder why you don't do it more often.

There's a vast array of simple, nonsensical things you might do: send a handmade card to work or to school, write an original How Wonderful You Are poem, tuck an inspirational message in a shoe, put a "Take the Day Off" coupon in an envelope and paste it on the bathroom mirror, surprise your kids by taking them out to lunch, have a one-on-one date, bring home a movie for the middle of the week, sprinkle knock-knock jokes in brief cases and book bags. Have age-appropriate joke books in the house and read them after the blessing at dinner. Look for the humor in everyday life. Eight-year-old Katy gave her favorite uncle Jack a soap on a rope for his birthday. He said, "I like it, but how will I wash my feet?"

Encourage humor in your family by designating a part of each day as the "Silliness Hour:" Roll on the grass, shake your body to music, make ugly faces, kick up your heels, lie on the floor and look for designs on the ceiling. Capture your family on video and become movie stars. Acts of silliness aren't silly; as a matter of fact, silliness helps you wind down, blow off steam, and get rid of pent-up energy. Children and adults need unstructured physical activity to get rid of the day's tensions. We all need room to move our bodies. Besides, it's healthy to dance, wiggle your feet, tap your toes, and giggle.

A good belly laugh gets your juices flowing. Make up silly verses, "I wish I was a willy wug." Kids get the hang of it quickly and will soon be reciting their own. Your teenagers will roll their eyes when you sing along to your favorite country song, but when they nickname you "Crazy Country Momma," you'll recognize it as a compliment. Have a laughing contest. Sit on the floor and pretend to laugh, make laughing noises, and watch the grouches and grumblers start laughing.

For the midweek blahs, a fresh approach is a perfect pick-me-up. Take a lesson from seven-year-old Jonathan. For two months straight he wore his Superman costume, then on Halloween he decided he wanted to go trick-or-treating as himself wearing a sweatshirt and jeans. Be original. Wear pajamas in the afternoon.

There's no better tonic than your loved one's laughter. Being spontaneous keeps a smile on your face. Life's so short—don't wait any longer. Sing loudly together: "Grab your coat and get your hat, leave your worries on the doorstep. Family life is sweet on the silly side of the street."

Plant a Family Garden

Six-year-old Amanda was playing at a friend's house when she overheard that her friend's teenage sister was grounded. Thinking this sounded fun, she ran home and asked, "Mom, when can I get grounded?" "Do you know that grounded means you can't go anywhere or talk to your friends?" I asked. "Shucks," she said, sounding disappointed. "I thought it meant I could dig in the dirt."

This conversation started me thinking about the benefits of "grounding." We all have those weeks when everyone in the family is restless, out of whack, bouncing off the walls. Digging in the dirt certainly calms you down and gets you on track—centered once again as you literally come down to earth. Pulling weeds, raking leaves, planting bulbs, sunflowers, sweet peas, pumpkins, and tomatoes is truly therapeutic. Thinking too much is tiring. In the garden, life slows down, you're working your body while resting your mind. Balancing brain waves by pushing a wheelbarrow empties the debris of your mind.

Years later, I did ground my teenage daughter because she needed an "attitude adjustment." The first time I told her the conditions of her "garden groundment," as we came to call it, she was baffled and pointed out, "None of my friends' parents do it this way." I explained to her that I didn't see garden grounding as punishment, but as a spiritual realignment, because in the garden, you discover the connection between nature and your soul. I explained to her that when I felt my attitude was getting out of line, spending time with flowers eased my anxieties, giving me a happier disposition.

It wasn't only my daughter that needed the pleasures of garden groundment. Once, when I was having a bad week, she said to me with such conviction that I took her advice, "You're grounded to the garden!" She was picking up that I was out of sorts, short tempered, cranky, and distracted. I was taking my frustrations out on her. After an hour of pruning the bushes, I could see the error of my ways and felt a shift in my perspective.

Garden groundment can include many different activities. Once I handed my daughter fifty daffodil bulbs to plant in a container before she could borrow the car. Other days, instead of ordering, "Go to your room," I said, "Read a book in the hammock until you feel better." On numerous occasions I told her, "Don't disturb me, I'm going to the hammock."

Being outside, touching the ground, getting dirt under your fingernails, walking barefoot, hanging a birdhouse, and planting seeds teach patience while giving you and your children a chance to reflect on what's going on internally. Watering the grass and watching seeds sprout gives each of you an experience of natural acts and consequences. Hugging and talking to trees is especially helpful when you're angry. You can pour out your meanness or your sorrow and the trees don't mind.

Tell your children that hugging and talking to a tree is more beneficial than groaning and whining. When they're finished, they'll feel and behave better. Tell them you're more likely to compromise when they're talking pleasant. Teaching these lessons is best accomplished when you set the example. If you're snappy, make a special effort to let your children know why you're turning to the garden. By talking to, hugging, and respecting the trees, they'll come to understand that they too have control over their actions.

Let Go of the Outcome

One of the most difficult lessons we learn in a family is how to care deeply about our loved ones and their lives while at the same time being able to detach ourselves from outcomes. It's a spiritual process of contributing your best, making your greatest effort, then turning the outcome over to your Higher Power. It's trusting in the process of life and putting the results in God's hands. Detaching from the outcome doesn't mean you don't care whether or not Molly gets selected for the band or that Christopher makes the rowing team, but rather that you cheerfully are open to the goodness and lessons as they evolve.

Your children have divine destinies, evolutionary tasks that you may not understand. You may have already had glimpses of your child's separateness from you, and as you watch their lives unfold, you grasp that imposing your will is not always prudent. You can help your third grader study her spelling, you can feed her a healthy breakfast, blow her a kiss and wish her good luck, but you can't take the spelling test for her. You can teach your son to hold a bat and tell him to keep his eye on the ball, you can even shout orders from the bleachers, but you can't run the bases for him.

Letting go is acting wisely, knowing that your loved ones are gaining life skills, as you did, directly from experience. Heather was a good student in high school, but her freshman year in college she dropped out of two classes and barely passed the others. Her parents expressed concern that she was socializing more than she was studying. They warned her of the consequences, then stepped back, and kept their fingers crossed. Heather was shy in high school and didn't have friends, now she was branching out, making friends, having fun, while hopefully gaining people skills and learning the value of time management.

As family members we must practice acceptance rather than resignation. We must accept the experience as it is and be creative with how we handle it. Gail married Bill five months after her husband of forty-seven years died. Her adult children were dumbfounded. When Bill moved into the family home, they were afraid that he was taking over. They were angry. They expressed doubts and voiced their disappointments. They said to their mother, "We love you, we stand by you, and if this is what you want, we'll accept it and be watching." Rather than jumping to conclusions and withdrawing, they're choosing to get to know Bill, finding out what makes him tick.

You mature spiritually when you accept the separateness of you and your loved ones. By acknowledging that you can't dominate their lives or control the outcome, you surrender your will to the Almighty. They, and you, are in God's hands. Like you, they're on a spiritual journey, learning lessons of the soul. By getting out of the way, kismet can come.

Celebrate with One Another

There's no better tonic than your loved ones' laughter.

Behave in a Friendly Fashion

Friendliness is a quality that isn't talked much about in family relationships, but I believe that conducting yourself in a friendly manner—especially toward your loved ones—will keep your family thriving.

Don't confuse friendliness with a phony "everything's hunky-dory" approach. Family life is not without its skirmishes and strife. Within every family there are personality differences, diverse points of view, misunderstandings, hard feelings, and dislikes. Yet even the most complicated relationships move in a more positive direction when addressed in a spirit of friendliness.

Friendliness is a quality of openness that lets your child, your spouse, your sister, or your brother know that even when you disagree you're still playing on the same team. Friendliness conveys to the other person that you're interested in them, believe in them, are behind them, and that you're willing to go the extra mile to make sure they are part of your life. Friendliness communicates the idea that you want to spend time getting to know them, hang out with them, find out how they're doing. Friendliness breeds good-natured cooperation. It's taking an honest look at what you can do together to tackle what difficulties you might be facing. It's a sense of joy, appreciation, and excitement that you're sharing a portion of your life with such funny, interesting, and complicated human beings.

We've all fallen short of this goal. As the song says, "You always hurt the ones you love, the ones you shouldn't hurt at all." We've dumped pain on each other and been on the receiving end of bad treatment. We've taken each other for granted. We've been cranky and preoccupied. We've snapped and been irritable. We all know that a little friendliness smooths the wrinkles, paves the way in a positive direction, yet sometimes we're lazy and don't bother to be pleasant. We've treated acquaintances and strangers with more consideration.

Marilyn scolded seven-year-old Jimmy for hiding his pet gerbil in his pocket. Her tone of voice was shrill and strident. She shook her finger and had a frown on her face. In front of his friends, she grabbed him by the sleeve of his jacket and told him to get in the car. She drove the carpool kids home and continued to reprimanded him. Then in the parenting workshop that evening she complained that her son never sits still.

When we treat our loved ones poorly it affects everything. They feel anxious and so do we. So how can you behave in a friendly fashion when you're overwrought and having a bad day? By wanting to and recognizing that you too will benefit when you do, because you'll feel better when you're congenial and easy going.

Friendliness teaches children that the world is a positive place. When you're friendly toward your children, they grow up knowing they can trust you. With a friendly manner you can say what's on your mind and they'll be willing to listen. You can give feedback, direction, and correction as long as your style is tactful. Children strive to cooperate when you treat them as you would your best friend.

Be Lighthearted

When I'm asked by clients or by families who attend my workshops for tips on how to improve their family life, I give them my very best advice: When attending to family matters, do it with a light heart. A light heart is full of love and promotes harmony. Family life is too important to be taken seriously—even when you're angry! It's best for you and your relationships if you're lighthearted about what's bugging you.

Your youngest lets the puppy sleep on your freshly washed bedspread, your daughter decides she can't live without a tattoo, your son's vice principal insists that you come for a parent conference, and your husband doesn't understand why you don't want to take another summer vacation hiking the back country. What else can you do but be lighthearted? You could rant, rave, pull out your hair, and clench your teeth and your fists; you could threaten to run away from home, or ground the kids for six months, but what good does it do you to get so uptight? After all, you have a problem that needs a solution, and something else will need fixing tomorrow. If it comes naturally to be strict and severe, perhaps you were raised that way. Was it good for you?

It takes true guts and maturity to approach life's annoyances while remaining lighthearted. You can say no, put your foot down, and keep your heart open. You can groan, moan, complain, protest, and still be lighthearted. You can remain centered while finding solutions. You can stay balanced while handling the crisis. You'll instill good will when you do.

Sternness is appropriate in some occasions. For example, you're on the phone and want the kids to quiet down immediately; or you're sitting in church, and you expect your children to stop whispering. A stern look lets them know you mean business, but it loses its effectiveness when it becomes your temperament. When your face is constantly contorted and frowning and your heart is closed, it poisons you child's inclination to cooperate with you. A stern look and a strict philosophy may get your children to follow your instructions for a while, but it won't get you a warm, close relationship. As soon as you turn your back, they'll gravitate toward the parent who is lighthearted.

James is one of those strict-type fellows. He wants the closets, the garage, the yard, the car, the dishwasher, the laundry room, the pantry, in fact the entire house, orderly and neat. He sternly reminds his wife, his kids, and the visiting cousins to put things back, pointing out what they left out of place. The kids are obedient, but his wife prefers to be playful while getting her jobs done. Even though she knows an orderly house is important to her husband, it isn't the most crucial thing. Sure, she likes to keep the house neat, but what matters the most to her is that her children are glad to be with her.

Admit Your Quirks

Have you ever sat around the dinner table with your mother, father, brother, sister, aunts, uncles, cousins, spouse, children, nephew, and nieces, and noticed what a diverse, unusual, precious bunch of characters are sitting with you? If you haven't noticed the distinguishing features of your relatives you might want to take a closer look next time you're together. Or, better yet, imagine that you're sitting together right now. Stand back and look at each of them as if they were characters in a movie. Watch what they do, and listen closely to what they say. Notice their quirks, their mannerisms, the silly little traits that make them who they are. Aren't they entertaining? Aren't you glad that you have them in your life? Wouldn't life be dull without them? You could probably fill a novel with the skeletons in your combined closets. Pay attention to the drama and don't overlook comedy. Academy Awards have been given for less acting skills then your relatives exhibit.

Admitting that you and your relatives have quirks is healthier and much more lively than sweeping them under the rug. Aunt Lily may smoke cigars and wear black lace stockings, Granddad Joseph may have a seamy past, but colorful true-life characters are more entertaining than "pretend-everything's-perfect, put-on-a-front" families. Covering up leads to coldness and distance from one another, while openly acknowledging family secrets prevents them from swelling into symptoms of dysfunction.

Many times you've asked yourself, "why do I need these people anyway?" After all you don't have much in common except genes, history, and a few things you'd like to forget. Then, just when you think of disassociating from the entire clan, you get slightly sentimental and decide they're not that bad. Besides, there's something strangely comforting about relatives who know where you come from. It's as if you are looking in a mirror, and through it you can see what you absolutely don't want to be. Doug's irresponsible father comes to family gatherings, but is never pleasant. He smokes even though he has emphysema; he drinks even though his liver is shot. But Doug is polite and does what he can. He says, "Seeing what my father has become has made me determined not to become like him." We all have flaws. It's good to know what they are, so, like Doug, you can address them.

Our lives are interwoven. You can take what fits, leave the rest, and be good-natured about it all. Being part of a family gets you in touch with your capacity to love. It's doesn't take much to appreciate someone who's perfect—it doesn't require much love on your part. But appreciating someone with a full range of idiosyncrasies is really something worth bragging about. That's the nature of Divine Love— loving someone who isn't perfect.

Appreciate Feelings

You have within you a wide, bright rainbow of feelings. Everyone does—boys, girls, moms, dads, babies, teens, and grandparents. Feelings are like arms and legs; they're an important part of who you are. Like arms, legs, hands, feet, and hair and eye color, you were given feelings by grand design. They add dimension and sparkle, give you sensitivity and spunk, and make your life richer. Just as you wouldn't chop off your leg or poke out your eye, you don't want to cut off, repress, or suppress your feelings. You don't want to poke fun at them, push them away, or hide them. Like legs and arms, feelings are handy to have; they serve a practical and marvelous purpose.

In order to use feelings effectively and appropriately, you need to be able to identify and be comfortable with them. When you know how your feelings work, you're able to allow your children management over their own. Young children actually use their feelings more reasonably than parents. Crying loudly when hurt, shrieking freely when mad, and smiling and wiggling when happy. Without knowing it, parents sometimes reinforce our culture's gender stereotypes, teaching boys that they should feel one way and girls should feel something else. "You shouldn't feel that way," "Don't cry," "Smile," "Don't be afraid," and "Be nice" are messages that place limitations on your child's emotional inner life. When children are told that what they're feeling is wrong, they lose their personal sense of reality, which wreaks havoc on their self-esteem and all their relationships. Just as everyone has a right to their own bodies and their own thoughts, everyone has a right to their own feelings.

You know how you become lethargic when you sit around all day without any exercise? It's the same when you deny what you're feeling. You get stagnant and lose your ability to know what you need and want; you lose your creativity. Exercising your physical and emotional prowess makes for a healthier human being. If you don't use your innate abilities, you'll be left pitifully underdeveloped.

Respect what you're feeling. Say to yourself, "It's okay to feel the way I do." If you're angry, feel it. Then choose what to do. Just as you choose whether to walk, skip, or run when you feel like moving, you can choose what to do when happy or sad.

Feelings left unattended are present just the same, often directing your relationships without your even knowing it. Healthy families allow feelings to point in a direction worth exploring. When you hear each other's feelings, you know each other better. Feelings, like rainbows, come and go quickly. At the end of your feelings comes a pot of pure gold—a new understanding, a clear focus, a new perspective; a sigh of relief—like calm after a storm.

Lighten the Atmosphere
with Laughter

Laughter is the not only the best medicine, it's also the best family therapy. Your kids and your mate will love it when you're goofy. Goofing off relieves anxiety and reduces stress. It's an antidote to family doldrums and a cure for strained encounters. If you can laugh without poking fun, teasing, or undermining, then you've discovered the cure for pent-up tension.

In distraught and troubled families, you can feel the tension in the air. They may make attempts at humor, but rather than lighten up the atmosphere, the humor is used to embarrass one another or to disguise cruel put-downs. On the other hand, happy families see the humorous side of life. They're able to laugh and giggle about the silly little things that happen each day.

Megan, the mother of three rambunctious boys, is known for her nonsensical sayings: "Time to do the chores, chores, chores, again! Let's get started; we've got complaining, pouting, moaning, whining, and work to get done." She uses funny voices to get the guys' attention and engage their willingness to help. Using her imagination, she's able to place the emphasis on the positive side of sibling relationships rather than on the fact that the kids are picking on each other: "Brothers fighting, fighting, fighting, equals loving, loving, loving." The first time she sang this little jingle the boys had been fighting for thirty minutes about whose turn it was to ride "shotgun." It works better than the other techniques she's tried to keep the kids from arguing. Megan says, "When I sing the 'Sibling Fighting Song,' my three boys band together as a cooperative unit to convince me how much they really don't love each other."

Laughter is also cheerful link between you and your spouse. It adds buoyancy to your alliance, making the trials and tribulations easier to bear. Without laughter, married life and parenting can be overtaken with drudgery and obligation. But with a touch of lightness and gaiety, you're able to take everyday struggles in stride.

Add a hint of whimsy to your clothes. Lee makes fanciful ties for her husband Dave. Dave coaches Little League, and his sporty collection brings enthusiastic raves from his cohorts. Be good-natured about your surroundings. When Katy went overboard decorating with an angel theme, her husband Jim placed a red devil figurine in the corner of the living room for "balance."

You don't have to be playing practical jokes to add laughter to your routine. You don't have to do slapstick or be the clown. Expressing your cheerfulness in subtle, charming ways is magically infectious. Walk sprightly, hum a little ditty, paint the front door red. You can lighten the atmosphere by being your one-of-a-kind, original, silly little self.

Bestow Affection Daily

Have you ever seen families standing or sitting right next to each other, yet you sense an awkward distance between them? It's as if an invisible shield is protecting them from one another. Next time you're at the airport, watch the various styles that families use to greet each other. You'll be able to tell who feels comfortable showing affection and who doesn't like it very much. Some hug and kiss with ease; others look downright clumsy. Some shake hands, while others pat each other on the shoulders. Still others lean forward like an inverted "V" barely brushing each others checks. Some make little puckering sounds and kiss the air. Some smile and wave hello, some squeal with delight as soon they spot each other, others simply nod in recognition. Have you ever wondered why there are such different styles?

Healthy families are comfortable with affection and exchange it daily. No one ever outgrows the need for human touch—a hug, a hand squeeze—yet sadly, too many families seem to function without it. It's not all that uncommon for adults to be uncomfortable showing affection to the ones who matter most.

Maybe it's because as children they grew up being touched harshly, and now, as adults, they associate touching with getting hurt. Maybe because of all the sexual innuendoes bombarding people everywhere, folks don't know how to touch without being sexual. Maybe people think that showing affection is mushy, silly, and unnecessary. Or perhaps they don't like the vulnerability that accompanies tenderness. Whatever the reason, if you'd like to be more open with affection, but are so out of practice you don't know where to begin, here's an exercise to get you started:

The next time someone touches your hand, be sure to watch what happens. The next time someone calls you an affectionate little love name, pay close attention to what goes on inside of you. Notice that when someone touches you warmly, your whole body feels better, you relax, and are less uptight. When someone calls you by a love name your heart melts, you're smiling, skipping, cooperating. Suddenly the job you were dreading is doable.

Affection is the reassurance that you're loved. A gentle hug, holding hands, walking arm and arm, are all heartwarming gestures that say "you're special to me." If your family adores you and shows it, you feel lovable. But if you don't get enough affection, you're left with aching doubts. When you know you're loved, you walk with a spring in your step, and there's a twinkle in your eye.

Welcome Bad Moods Too

Amanda announced to me one afternoon, "I've been denying myself my bad mood all day." "What do you mean?" I asked. "I've been putting pressure on myself not to be in a bad mood and that's making me nervous," she explained; "I'm just going to enjoy my bad mood for the rest of the night." She said this so cheerfully that I could see she was on the right track.

As Amanda figured out, it's paradoxical that when you allow yourself your bad mood, you feel better than if you put pressure on yourself to get over it. So don't deny yourself your dark moods. Don't cajole your kids to put on a happy face so that *you'll* feel better. Nothing is worse than being forced to smile so that you look acceptable. In some of my favorite pictures of young children they are caught with sober faces, when so much depth of character shines through. Forcing someone to appear as something they are not does not make for good mental health.

Families are made up of fragile human beings who get moody, irritable, sullen, cranky, mad, and depressed. Everyone is entitled to be cranky—including you. Unfortunately some folks think that they need to hide their moods or masquerade as if they're feeling chipper. That only makes the mood last longer. Say to your loved ones: "I'm going through my snarly phase." "I'm feeling cranky, ornery, and cross. And to top it off I have a sore throat." Allow them the same privilege too. As long as you warn people that you're in a bad mood, you don't need to talk about the details until you're ready to share. Everyone deserves the pleasure of a bad mood; besides, it's therapeutic to discover that bad moods are not permanent conditions.

Bad moods can come in the morning or in the middle of the day. Moods come for a good reason or for no reason at all. It's how you greet them that determines whether they take over, ruin your day, or disappear. When moods come upon you—or the ones you love—it's best to just let them be for a while. They may pass without need for any intervention. If they don't, a change of scenery, a warm bath, or dancing can be suitable cures.

Add a Healthy Dose of Excitement

The New Kids on the Block were appearing at the Washington State Fair, and ten-year-old Amanda and her best friend Amy were dreaming of going. I had mixed feelings since the concert was on a school night, but after talking it over with Amy's dad, we agreed they deserved a change of pace. They were thrilled. We stood in line for over an hour, found our seats, and eagerly watched the crowd. Suddenly everyone jumped to their feet screaming, shaking, dancing, and crying as the musicians ran on stage. The music was deafening—excitement was in the air. Amanda's and Amy's eyes were as big as saucers; they'd never experienced such pandemonium. They stood frozen for about three minutes until Amanda looked up at me and said, "Mom, is it okay if I scream?" "Yes, honey," I said, "that's what concerts are for." "Amy," she said, "it's okay if we scream." And so they screamed, danced, laughed, and wiggled for two hours. Their first concert, an occasion I'll never forget. "Thanks so much for taking us," they said over and over; "It was better than the rides."

Excitement comes in many forms: concerts, horseback rides, hiking, flying kites, water-balloon fights, or sharing a beautiful spot in nature. It might be taking your kids someplace they've never seen before. Or going for a walk just before the sun comes up, building sand castles, or blowing bubbles. It might be arriving home from school and finding your parents came home early just to spend an afternoon with you. It might be teaching your kids how to read a recipe, to shop for the groceries, or to cook a casserole and a flaming dessert. Suzanne, whose four children are grown with children of their own, says, "It's experiences I want to share with my children, grandkids, daughters-and sons-in-law."

Give your family exciting experiences. Discover new things; leap into arenas you've never explored before. Play Mozart, and go to the symphony. Sing in the shower, and play a sing-along tape in the car. Let your son pick out the paint for his bedroom furniture—paint it together and show him how to clean out the brushes. Don't cling to the things you know best—be courageous and experiment. You'll get stodgy if you never try anything new. Show your daughter how to hold a hammer and use a drill. How about trying bowling, fishing, roller skating? Read poetry, plan a makeup party for your teenage daughter, or take your teenage son pretend shopping for fancy sports cars and teach him to read a blue book. Don't let your family stagnate in pools of apathy and boredom.

Reach out and meet your neighbors. Make an ice cream cake and plan an Easter parade. Get to know each other. When the house is a mess, the laundry piled high, the refrigerator needs cleaning, and you're feeling restless, it's time to venture beyond your neighborhood. Take a trip on a train or a bus, and let your kids teach you to read a map. Plan a field trip to the park on the other side of town. Ask your children's friends and their parents to go along.

The more experiences you share, the more well-rounded and educated you'll all become. Besides, if you're having a good time together when the kids are young, when you're old they'll still want to come around because you're so much fun.

Take Pictures

Have you ever sat on the floor looking through piles of old family photographs and suddenly caught a glimpse of your mother when she was your age and become aware of a part of her you hadn't known before? Have you ever seen a snapshot of your parents with their arms around each other? Looking closely, you can see the love shining on their faces. Have you had the pleasure of getting to know your ancestors through old photo albums? Have you looked at your baby pictures? Shared them with your kids?

Whether your pictures are stored randomly in shoe boxes, organized by vacations in albums, or arranged by the year on video or laser disc, family photographs tell stories that words can't express. They hold lost memories, contain family history. Pictures of birthdays, graduations, weddings, vacations, summer camp, and babies on blankets bring sweet recollections. Your little girl's first birthday, your son's first Halloween costume, their first day of school. "First" moments come and go quickly. Capturing the occasion on film or video gives you a sensorial keepsake. Whether it's a wedding album or newborn baby snapshots, photographs let you revisit the occasion and the feelings that went with it. You're likely to be pleasantly surprised, and get goose bumps and shivers, because not only will the picture jog your memory, it will awaken the love you felt at the time.

After your children are grown and move away from home, you'll have these pictures in common. They're entertainment at family gatherings. Sorting through your photos, pasting them in albums, or organizing the videos are great ways to stay close. After all, no one, not even your best friends, will enjoy "oohing" and "ahhing" and reminiscing more than your family: "I remember that." "Remember when we went to the lake?" "Look how beautiful you were." "Look at your hairstyle." "Where did you get those pants?" Pictures remind us of what we have in common.

Keep a camera and rolls of film handy. There's always an opportunity to catch your family being themselves. You don't need to pose them or plan out the picture, just let them be natural. Don't force smiles. Try taking close-ups of feet and hands, and then at your next gathering, let your gang play a game identifying feet and hands. Take pictures of the everyday things. Claudia took a picture of her grandson learning to stand at the potty. "It's a significant event in a little boy's life which isn't often recorded," she said. "He's very proud of that picture."

Take pictures using the same pose, the same location, or the same time of year. Kris and Ron have been taking pictures of their four sons climbing the same tree in the park for the past fourteen years. They frame each picture and hang in the den. It's a history and a conversation piece. Henry and Alice organized three identical albums as gifts for their grown kids. Keep photos of family hanging on your refrigerator door and you're sure to keep smiling.

Permit Downtime

The organization and elbow grease that it takes to keep your family running calls for skills that even high-paid executives haven't mastered. If you're like most American families, your "to do" list is longer than the hours in your day, and more complicated than a physics equation. You're a wage earner, taxi driver, chef, consultant, volunteer, accountant, psychologist, coach, nurse, and domestic engineer. Is there any doubt that you're exhausted and need a break?

Puttering around is the ultimate stress reducer, because when nothing's planned or expected, you don't have to focus on the outcome, and you don't have to push for results. Dawdle away the afternoon by rummaging through the books you've been meaning to read. Loaf on the couch. Twiddle your thumbs, and invite your honey and kids to join in. These days kids lives are chock full of so many activities and studies that they barely have time to be children. Their souls need nurturing too. Encourage them to "go outside and stare at clouds." Pretending in a tree house, drawing chalk sidewalk pictures, catching bugs, and playing tag are all methods of soul rejuvenation. Teenagers, too, need downtime to lie on their bed, look in the mirror, "chill," and talk to friends. When you allow downtime for yourself and other family members, you give yourselves the advantages that come with being bored. It's during down time that you discover the glory of imagination and doodling. Doing nothing is often the most creative time of all. It's when ideas and inspiration incubate.

When was the last time your family frittered away a day? Have you ever lounged around for a whole week? Take a vacation from your chores. If you can't go quite that far, try leaving at least one task undone. Instead of working hard around the house before you relax, loaf first, and tackle your projects later. You may be surprised to find that taking a break first gives you a spurt of energy so that you get the chores done in half the time. And if you don't, it really doesn't matter because the unmade beds will still be there tomorrow. Give your kids a "No Chore Today Coupon" and let them have an easy day, too.

Dinah said, "I only want to do what I want to do, at my own rhythm and, right now, I don't even know what that would be. I don't want to fold the laundry, give a speech tonight, or pay my bills. I want to sit and stare." Taking it easy, going at your own pace, doing nothing are the best alternative medicines for restoring balance to your life. If you must do something, do one thing at a time. Josie, the mother of four, has been known to spend an entire day in her robe. Her kids no longer question what she's doing because she's told them, "I'm having a pajama party." Occasionally she invites her mother and friends over for a slumber party.

Take your family on a do-nothing mini vacation. Sip lemonade, sit in a lawn chair, and watch the flowers grow. You'll bestow upon your kids the pleasure of living with relaxed, balanced, easygoing parents.

Grant the Freedom to Grow

Families are constantly changing. Babies change almost by the hour. They grow physically and mentally so rapidly, you can notice the differences daily. But babies aren't the only "change artists"; every human being is growing, evolving, becoming who they're meant to be. Everyone in your family is evolving, growing, tackling new things, and mastering life skills.

Change is the norm. If you expect family life to remain the same, you're in for a quite a jolt. As a parent with a few years of experience under your belt, you know that as soon as you've adjusted to one stage, the kids are in the middle of another. In the thick of change, growth can seem painstakingly slow, but looking back, you realize how well your family is growing and surviving. During the years between when your one-year-old learns to walk and that same child learns to drive, you've conquered countless ups and downs. It takes sixteen years until a child is old enough to drive the car, yet it seems to happen overnight. And although you like the independence that her mobility brings, sometimes you wish you could just hold her safely on your lap.

Coping with the changes that come with adolescence is high on most parents' "dread list" You know your teen needs freedom, but how much and when you're not quite sure. Just as the hair style you wore at fifteen won't look good on your daughter today, the curfew you had as a teenager is likely to be outdated. As your son pushes for more freedom, if you're willing to side step power struggles and polish your negotiating skills, your son or daughter will look to you as a leader rather then avoid you as a disciplinarian.

An enormous part of adolescence is finding out what the world is all about. If you're not allowing your teen to make his own decisions, he won't have much life management experience under his belt. If your daughter hasn't had any room to spread her wings, she might rebel or remain so sheltered she can't succeed on her own. Give teenagers plenty of freedom by extending the boundaries. It's normal that your teenager will spend more time with friends than with you; granting the freedom to grow means that you let them. It also includes honestly negotiating the bottom line: "You can go to the party if you call when you get there and call just before you leave to come home."

In the process of growth, we often have the mistaken notion that we ought to do it perfectly—get it right the first time. Whether you're trying to change a bad habit, learning to tie your shoes, studying a foreign language, learning to drive a car, or struggling to parent a teen, no one gets it perfect all the time. Just as you learned to tie your shoes with considerable practice and frustration, whatever change unfolds, there's defeat and victory marching with it. A parade of opportunities is advancing your family's way. You'll gain mastery when you greet them with an open mind.

Make Work and Chores Meaningful

Eleven-year-old Amanda chose emptying the dishwasher and taking out the garbage as her chores, but after a couple of months she was complaining, "I don't like emptying the dishwasher—it's boring. Let me do the laundry instead," she pleaded. "You're too young to do the laundry," I protested. "I can do it if you show me how," she insisted. We had this conversation so many times that finally I caved in and delivered a lecture in the art of separating whites from colors, the nuances of water temperature, and the complex operating settings of the washer and dryer. Thinking to myself that this would be so complicated, she would gladly return to the more manageable job.

To my astonishment, she liked doing her own laundry and took over the supervision of her clothes (I did my own) and the towels. When Grandma came to visit, she taught Amanda stain management—which Amanda says, "Mom knows nothing about." Occasionally when Amanda was bogged down with school obligations, the laundry would pile up and I would do a load. "Mom if you can't do it right, don't do it," she would complain. I admit it, I don't know how red socks sneak in with the whites. (I'm good at emptying the dishwasher though.) Moral of the story: Do work you're good at.

From kids to adults, folks do better with work that is meaningful. Once Amanda had conquered the dishwasher, she was bored and ready for a bigger challenge. Doing the laundry had personal significance because she likes her clothes spiffy. It was great for me too because I didn't have to say a word about how many clean towels she used. And Amanda received plenty of recognition from friends and relatives who were impressed that an eleven-year-old could manage the responsibility.

Ask your kids what contribution they'd be willing to make to the daily operations of your family. Listen to what they're saying about chores, and notice which ones they're resisting. Pay attention to their interest and skill level and brainstorm to see if you can find a match. Doing the same chore over and over again gets boring for some kids; others prefer the repetition. Try to find chores that give your child personal satisfaction while building self esteem. Let them move from one thing to another. Eleven-year-old Ellis traded mowing the lawn for typing mailing lists into the computer, becoming his dad's capable at-home office assistant.

Instead of insisting that they do chores, "whether you like it or not," participate with them in finding a chore that is satisfying. By experiencing this process at home, your young adult will understand the importance of meaningful work and will be able to apply these skills in locating a satisfying job. Eventually this will lead to a fulfilling career.

Use these techniques with yourself too. If you work outside the home at a job you can't bear, your frustration is bound to spill over. Does your work support your family life or are long hours eroding your family life? Set a personal goal to find work that is satisfying and compatible with family life. (By the way, every kid needs to have the joy that comes with running a vacuum cleaner. Point out how nice it feels after a carpet is vacuumed or the floor mopped.) Share the chores, talk about the pleasures, and let everyone have a voice.

Greet One Another with a Smile and Cheery Hello

Well-known family therapist Virginia Satir says: "Every word, facial expression, gesture, or action on the part of a parent gives the child some message about self-worth." For years, parents have been concerned about their children's self-esteem. Parents know that children with positive self-regard have a better start in life. They make friends easily and are better equipped to face life's challenges. Feeling good about oneself, not in a pompous way, but rather in a confident way, is the stabilizing ingredient in your child's ability to enjoy life and succeed. All events going on in your family, beginning with the way you greet each other each morning and ending with the way you say good night are registered within each family member—from babies to teenagers and adults. And, particularly for the kids, what those interactions are like can affect their sense of self-esteem. When one member of your household gets the flu or comes down with a cold, everyone is concerned that they might catch it too. It's a legitimate concern because if Johnny has the flu, the measles, or a runny noise, his sister will probably get it too. It's the same with the grouchies. If day after day, Dad or Mom wake up in a bad mood, with nothing pleasant to say, chances are his or her mood will be contagious.

It feels better to wake up to a pleasant greeting. "Good morning," said with a smile paints a heavenly mood over your household. Abruptly shouting, "Get up!" puts nerves on edge and brings bad vibes into your dwelling. It doesn't do much for family life to have negativity floating in the air. Self-esteem is developed in small, simple actions. Beginning with how you start your day. If you snap orders like a drill sergeant to get yourself and the kids out the door on time, perhaps you need to reexamine your routine or rearrange your schedule.

I often ask five- and six-year-olds to describe their parents. I get the most revealing answers. Many of them say their parents don't smile enough, and spend their time barking orders: "Don't forget your lunch," "Wipe your feet," "Don't leave your books in the hallway." "Clean up your room," "Hurry up, you're late." How do you want your children to describe you? Rushing around with a frown your face? Or cheerful and taking life lightly?

The quality of your life depends on your attitude. It's how you handle the everyday hassles that separates contented folks from the complainers. Do you nag and criticize or do you whistle as you're working? Do you sing instead of snapping? When you take life lightly, you know that looking for the humor makes even the most exasperating incidents easier to handle. When the kids are eating spoonfuls of peanut butter directly from the container and the kitchen's full of crumbs and finger smudges, it's how you respond that matters. You can tear your hair out and threaten, or you can grab a spoon and dig in. You can lock yourself in a closet, scold, and plead or you can count to ten and say nicely, "Now clean up, please."

Be Generous with Appreciation

Appreciation is the heavenly way of seeing, the holy way of responding. It honors the eternal force that brings you together, opening your mind and heart to the spiritual journey that you're sharing. It's deep gratitude for the unseen tie that keeps you joined. Appreciation reflects the deep understanding that God resides within each of you. Showing your thankfulness through your demeanor, words, and actions is your earthly celebration of the Almighty's Love.

Appreciation is a heart overflowing with joy—a contagious effervescence for all that they are and all that you're sharing. Appreciation is taking delight in your son's unique observations, your daughter's loving spirit, your partner's kind consideration when you were feeling sick. It's noticing the little things—the twinkle in his eye, the softness of her hair, the special characteristics that make them who they are. It's the melting of your heart when your baby pats you on the cheek. It's the blessings of walking through life with these wonderful people.

A pat on the back, an encouraging thumbs up, a nod of acknowledgment, or a smile of recognition means so much coming from you: your son wants you to notice how much effort he's making; your daughter needs you to appreciate how hard she's trying, your partner thrives when you acknowledge the work she puts in, and your parents crave understanding of what they have given.

"I appreciate you" is a song for the soul. Show it and say it. Don't assume that your loved ones know how much you cherish them. Even though they know you very well, they can't read your mind. You have to put your appreciation into words and show it through your actions. Hearing Dad say, "I love you," never gets old. Hearing Mom say, "Thank you," is always meaningful.

Appreciating each other keeps your relationship positive. If all you do is complain and point out shortcomings, resentments will start piling up. Walls of resentments take years to remove. It's okay to talk about annoying habits and tendencies as long as you also bring to the discussion a sense of appreciation. You can be straight with one another and appreciative at the same time. You can incorporate the difficult and promote good relations. It's a little like being a customer service representative. Think of yourself as "family service representative." Deal with complaints in a straight manner. Give your undivided attention and say, "I appreciate the fact that we are working it out together." Make your tone friendly; smile, and stay upbeat.

Appreciation is knowing that you're all pulling together for the greater good. In all that you do and all that you say, show your appreciation for each other.

Encourage Natural Talents

Have you ever noticed that some members of your family are like tulips? They have flair and independence, you just can't arrange them. Like tulips they stand out in a bunch. Tulips add pizazz to any bouquet. They're determined to be who they are. Perhaps you know a relative who fits this description. Perhaps this is your child. Perhaps it's you.

God has a plan for everyone. You may not believe this is true for you, but think of it this way: As a mother or a father, don't you want the very best for your children? Wouldn't you move heaven and earth to keep them safe, make their dreams come true? Well, don't you think the Divine is doing the same for you?

If you're following the national trend, you may have adopted the bad habit of overlooking your gifts in favor of improving upon your shortcomings. And if you're doing it to yourself, you're probably also unintentionally tying to improve others. Yes, we all have weaknesses and shortcomings, but more importantly, we all have distinctive knacks and talents. Human beings, like tulips, are spectacular when allowed to discover and develop their genius. Just like comparing one tulip to another serves no useful purpose, comparing your children to each other is futile. So is comparing yourself to your older sister— it's devastating to your self-esteem and spirit. Following your dreams and aptitudes is sufficient for finding your niche. Given opportunity, propensities ripen.

At a young age, Kayla watched Olympic ice skaters on television and pretended her dolls were champions. Her parents encouraged her interest and gave her lessons. Her instructor encouraged her to perform in regional exhibitions. Kayla's skating was adequate, but her costumes were magnificent. She spent months designing each one and over the years, other skaters sought her advice. Through pursuing her interest in skating, she uncovered a natural bent for costume design. Fortunately for Kayla, she wasn't compared to the more talented skaters. She was appreciated for her unique flair and as an adult is a costume designer.

Put away your measuring stick and don't compare. Far too many talents are crushed underfoot before they've had a chance to develop because of comparisons and competition. Don't measure your children by the successes of others. Competition makes children give up and stop trying. Comparing yourself to others is not an accurate yard stick.

Encourage your children's talents while pursuing your own. Don't stomp on your dreams by saying, "I'd like to write poetry, but I'm not capable like others." You never know where you'll end up when you follow your leanings. Inspire yourself and your children to excellence by comparing the headway you make this month with where you were last month. You can reinforce talents by competing with yourself, not others: "You did four last time; now can you do six?" Give your children a sense of adequateness and a vision of themselves by cheering their—and your—natural talents.

Turn Off the Television

I read a startling statistic recently that said that a typical household has two television sets both turned on an average of six hours each day. This isn't good for family life. I've known families who have nothing to talk about except the details of their favorite soap opera scandal. I've heard families argue about talk show guests. I've known others who kept two televisions blaring during Thanksgiving dinner so that they wouldn't miss a single football play. These families are suffering from media overdose. Is yours?

Whenever I speak to parents, I hear their concerns that kids are growing up too soon. Even very young kids know what's stylish, sexy, and hip; they seem to have lost their precious innocence. Commercials influence everything from food choices to music preferences. Raised on daily doses of violence, sexual innuendo, and sarcastic humor, children incorporate these values as part of their belief system. Is the television the focal point of your living room, family room, or bedroom? Are your children more influenced by the remote control than by your guidance?

Too much TV is harmful on many levels. Television overload is frequently an indication of boredom or exhaustion. We all need to veg out occasionally, but there are more exciting ways to unwind then zoning out in front of the jabber box. The vibration alone is enough to give you the heebie-geebies and put your nerves on edge. Television interferes with your abilities to interact with each other. There's not much room for flowing conversations when you're engrossed in the tube.

Television stifles creativity because it doesn't allow you to use your imagination, like reading. While reading a book, you imagine what the characters look like; with television, nothing, including the gory details, is left to the imagination. Your involvement with reading makes a difference in a child's ability and enthusiasm for learning. Don't wait until your children understand words to read to them. Intelligence develops through looking and talking about picture books, too. Thinking for one's self is enhanced through reading, particularly folk tales. Use stories such as "The Emperor's New Clothes" or "The Little Engine That Could" to impart values.

Storytelling is good at bedtime, on road trips, around a campfire and at family gatherings too. At extended family gatherings, the Edelsons, the Harpers, and the Rileys play the story telling game. Everyone participates. Grandpa Harper usually begins the story by saying, "When I was a boy, I had to walk fourteen miles to see your Grandma Mary. One Saturday after milking the cows I started toward her house when suddenly. . . ." He continues the story adding some truth here and some not-quite-truths there until he's tired of telling, then he passes the story to Grandma Mary or Uncle Peter to continue the tale. Each person plays and adds either a pretend or real story line. This activity can go on for hours. One summer at the lake, each night after dinner, they picked up the story where they left off the night before.

Kids adore playing board games with their parents. It's a great way to bond with each other. Remember: when you turn off the television you turn on the imagination. Playing, reading, and talking together are energizing; it's family bonding at its best.

Eat Your Meals Outdoors

According to the ancient Chinese tradition of feng shui, eating your meals at a round table brings you heavenly blessings. What a glorious event, dining with your loved ones at a round table, soaking up the blessings. What more blessings come from sitting in a circle, eating meals outdoors. Oh, what pleasant ambiance! Outdoors, breakfast, lunch, and midnight snacks are transformed into gatherings that no one skips.

Let's face it, after years of mealtime routines, even the most sociable families get lackadaisical about eating together. Mom wearies of cooking, Dad tires of cleaning up, and the kids ignore the conversations. But take your meals to the front porch or picnic on a blanket and magically everyone is telling jokes and laughing.

You put pizazz into mealtime when you eat outdoors. Breakfast cooked over an outdoor grill, sandwiches built while sitting on a bench, supper next to a tree, will guarantee a banquet they'll remember. Kids are more willing to pitch in with preparation and clean up when they're having fun.

If it's snowing and you can't go outside, there are other ways to liven up your dining. Ann and David and their two children, Kelly and Mark, were absorbed in family dinner conversation when out of the blue, Ann announced "I'm going to be Kelly tonight" and began imitating eight-year-old Kelly's mannerisms. David followed her lead and said, "Well then, I'm going to be Mark," and he pretended he was his five-year-old son. Catching on quickly, the youngsters joined the charade. Trading places at the table, they switched identities. Kelly declared, "I'm Mom." Mark piped up, "I'm Dad." The family plunged into their roles and played their parts throughout the entire meal. It was outstanding impersonation.

"It's enlightening to see yourself through your children's eyes," Ann told me later, "They sure have our number and personalities down pat. Our kids can unmistakably mimic us."

The children enjoyed their parents antics. They too were flabbergasted at how well their parents knew them. They like the game and often ask to play "put yourself in the other person's place." "It isn't threatening," says Ann, "because we aren't trying to prove anything by it and we don't hurt or embarrass each other."

However you choose to make mealtimes special, make sure that when you gather you acknowledge your good fortune. Next time you're eating together, sit in a circle, and gently hold hands. Look gently into those dear faces. Aren't you thankful these beloved ones are part of your life? Take a moment, smile, and tell them so. Saying a prayer, or partaking in a quiet moment, brings your awareness to your precious ones gathered at the table. A mealtime blessing said by rote becomes artificial and turns phony. But a blessing said with awareness is a boon for the soul.

Extend Your Family Circle

Your family extends in many directions. There's your biological family, your chosen family, and your spiritual family. Whether you know it or not, you're always creating family. Surely you must have made a friend to whom you said, "You're closer than my sister," or "You're like a mother to me," or "I consider you my brother." We're always creating family that can include, but is not limited to, our biological families.

Think of your family in terms of not just one circle, but many. In the center of a piece of paper write your name. Around your name draw five concentric circles. On the circle closest to your name write the names of the people that you consider to be your strongest allies—the people with whom you have a soul connection. On the next circle write the names of the people that you care deeply about—the people who have a permanent place in your heart. On the next circle write the names of the people who are important to you. On the next circle write the names of people who you want to keep in your family circle, but for whatever reason you're not completely in tune with. You may add as many circles as you like, placing your friends, relatives, and acquaintances as you choose.

When you think of the person, ask yourself: where do they stand in relationship to me. Don't get caught up on where you *think* they *should* belong, but rather focus on how it seems to you. Follow your intuition. You can move the names from one circle to the other, depending on your circumstances. For example, as a baby your mother might have been in the inner circle, but as a teenager she probably moved to the outer edges.

This is your extended family circle. Look at the people who are closest to you—this is your inner family circle—the people you want to give the biggest chunk of your energy, time, love, and commitment. These are the people who are really there for you. Notice where you placed your biological relatives. Some may have earned a place in your inner circle; others may be on the periphery.

Your most meaningful relationships may not always be with biological family members. Your biological family may be in your circles but on the edges; you aren't in sync with them, yet you don't want to throw them out of your life. Friends often become chosen family. With them you experience being loved, heard, and fully seen.

Your inner circle is often made up of your spiritual companions because they help you embrace the higher ideals of gentleness, compassion, and creativity. This special group are the ones you tell your accomplishments to and they share your sense of pride and happiness. Hopefully, each member nurtures, and, in turn, is nurtured, appreciates and is appreciated. Hopefully, it's your inner circle who empathizes with you in your moments of disappointment and loss. With these people you can laugh, cry, sing, and be discouraged. With these people you can be yourself. You're loved in full measure, not because you're perfect, but because in their eyes you are truly precious.

Frolic, Romp, and Play

Someone once said that there are two things to aim for in life: first, to get what you want; and after that, to enjoy it. This certainly applies to family life. You wanted a family; now you can take pleasure in the fact that you've got next of kin. You can luxuriate in the miracle that you have dependents, people who are looking to you to show them the way. So now it's time to enjoy the family you've got. My suggestion is to devote ten minutes in the morning, afternoon, and evening to play. Tickle the little ones, flirt with your spouse, and giggle all together.

Family life, at its all-time best, is lived with playfulness. It's your attitude that makes the difference. You can live in a gloom and doom circus or romp in a festival of delight. The smile on your face and the twinkle in your eye can turn mowing the lawn, sweeping the walk, and cleaning the garage from drudgery into jubilation. Frolic through the house with a spring in your step, wink at one another, and leap with excitement as you reunite at the end of the day. Your family won't know how happy you are to see them unless you show it! Let your guard down, kick up your heels, and proclaim your affection and enthusiasm.

Worry is threatening family life. Worrying has become such a national pastime that it's woven it's ugly way into our daily lives. For the sake of your loved ones, you have to stop fretting. If you're worrying about whether or not you're doing enough, your children are soaking it up, and they'll start believing they're a burden. Fussing and stewing does nothing positive for your family. Worry at work, if you must, then leave it there. Put on your solemn face in church if you think it's proper, but when you come home, wear your brightest demeanor.

Parents mistakenly think that unless they're worrying, fretting, and plotting, their children will never amount to much. I know parents who are worried about their kids getting accepted to the right college before they've started preschool. I know families who are so worried about outside influences that they assume the worst. If you find that you're too serious, drop the somber demeanor immediately, before it strangles you.

Now that Tim is a father, he remembers the importance of lightheartedness when he was growing up. "Humor and laughter had a significant place in our family interactions. Both parents loved to make us laugh, and it is one of the most endearing memories I have of them. My mother would put on little 'shows' while making dinner, using different voices to portray the characters. She was corny, but she always had me laughing."

To be a laughing, playful parent you have to incorporate fun into your schedule. If you tend to be on the somber side you can change things around by behaving cheerful. Try waking up to your favorite boogie-woogie music. At the end of the day take the family swimming. It's almost impossible to worry when you're splashing. Have you taught your child to whistle?

Cherish One Another

When you feel grateful to your family, you'll discover that you can't feel grateful enough. You cannot repay, but you can be grateful. It's through gratitude that your family is united.

Adjust Your Attitude as Needed

When I told a colleague that I was writing a book about families, he said to me, "I see that most families are just struggling to survive and don't have the time or energy to do wonderful things. I can honestly say that throughout my life, I haven't seen many families that enjoy each other. If I sound cynical, I guess I am."

A woman attending my "Parenting with Love and Laughter" workshop said, "I get a bit overwhelmed with all the stories I'm privy to, and I begin to look around and ask, 'Is anyone happy or at peace?' I don't mean to sound like sour grapes, but I've lived long enough, experienced enough, and seen enough to know that happy, well-adjusted families are few and far between. I don't mean to say that there aren't moments of joy and richness, even in the most dysfunctional of families, but I think the Walton, Cleaver, and Nelson families are figments of someone's hopeful imagination."

We live in a society that tends to view family life through a black-and-white lens: either you come from the happy Cleaver family or from a dysfunctional family. If you're labeled dysfunctional, then family relationships seem hopeless. If you're from a healthy family, then, like the Cleavers, you don't have any discord. This view of families is overly simplistic. Families are much more complex than these "either/or" views.

Are there any families that don't have problems? Of course not! Are families stressed beyond their limits? Yes. The good news is that in spite of all the pressures, thousands of families understand the link between a happy family life and overall satisfaction in life. Families are overcoming the obstacles with such determination that attitudes are changing. Fathers are playing a greater role in nurturing children. Both parents are involved at home and in the outside world. Happy relationships are beginning to take top priority. Instead of putting careers first, more and more parents are focusing on raising children and putting the needs of their family front and center. Families are finding new ways to be together—from flexible work hours to home offices to living with extended family and sharing childcare.

The concept of what it means to be a loving family has broadened. The traditional nuclear family with a mother and father at the helm is no longer the only sanctioned model. A positive, enriched family life centering on commitment and loving each other, regardless of how many relatives there are or aren't, is the model for the twenty-first century. Being there to raise your children is where it's at! Whether the head of the household is a single father, a married couple, a young widow, or a grandparent, the emphasis is no longer on tradition, it's on meeting the needs of children.

I'm hopeful that our attitude toward children and families will continue to become more inclusive. As that happens, our attitudes will impact our communities, agencies, institutions, schools, and corporations, so that we truly are a nation whose policies are humane and made with families in mind.

Pull Together in Tough Times

Family means being there for "your" people, whether the number is just two or twenty. This isn't exclusive to blood relatives; we all know of biological families without that bond. Biology can create the physical unit of a family, but it's pulling together in tough times that tightens our connection. We see examples of this when families disagree in beliefs or disapprove of one another's life styles, but still maintain a sense of family solidarity. Mark said, "There was no breach in the loyalty to one another outside our family. There may have been some big disagreements within our family, but that was considered private family business. No matter how much my sister and I bickered with one another, we defended each other outside the home."

It's in the trenches of life-altering traumas—serious illness, loss of job, death of a loved one, divorce, and other disappointments—that you discover what you're made of. Difficult events call for all the physical, emotional, and spiritual strength you can muster. Pulling together gives you character, shows the stuff you are made of. "The jolt of hard times was the impetus for us to come together," Roger says. "When Mom had a stroke, my brother, sister, and I put aside our differences to do what was best for our parents. The hard times force us to get on our knees and search deeper to rekindle our commitment."

No matter how close you are, even if you live side by side, you and your loved ones can be worlds apart. Gaps as infinite as the black holes, chasms as deep as canyons, can exist between you, but that doesn't mean you throw in the towel. We can learn to accommodate the differences. Virginia said, "A coworker spends most of her time complaining about family members. She isn't speaking to this one or she's mad at that one. They can't get together because someone is mad about something. It makes me so glad to have an extended family that loves enough to rise above our differences."

In spite of major disagreements, families are pulling together in extraordinary ways to face their problems with dignity, giving us all hope. When Scott confirmed that what his parents suspected was true, that yes, he was gay, his mother cried, his dad shook his head and stared at the floor, and his brother punched the air and said things he later apologized for. For days it was a roller coaster of tears and accusations, threats and innuendoes, and then it shifted. Scott said, "We agreed to disagree because what matters is that we love each other."

There are family matters that you can't do anything about. There will be family conversations that shake you to your toes. When you're in the middle of a stormy discussion, place your hands in your lap, palms up, and you'll be able to think rationally and keep your heart open. Remember—in every moment you can chose to close down and be hard or remain soft and generous of spirit.

After the commotion has quieted, as a family you can rejoice that you've survived. Each day with your family you're given opportunities to rise above your differences, pull together, forgive one another for our human frailties, and move forward. The question is always: "How can we love each other more?"

Respect Your Elders

Your parents, the elders of your family, have come a long way. They've endured much. They've made sacrifices for you. You may not understand them, like them, or approve of all they do; they may never fully understand you or approve of what you do, but that's not the point. The point is that they're your parents and did the very best they could for you in their circumstances. Don't ever forget that they have circumstances too—many of which you may never fully understand unless you've walked in their shoes.

Perhaps you and your parents struggled when you were growing up and the rift has never fully been repaired. Perhaps it never will be. But if you treat them with respect, emphasizing the positive they have done, you'll have peace of mind when they die, knowing that you did what you could to maintain a connection. By showing respect you won't be left dragging a bag of stale resentments and leftover guilt.

Respecting your parents, your grandparents, and the senior members of your family is a gift that shows how mature you are. When you show respect for your elders, the youngsters in your family learn to show respect for you.

Respect is given through the little things you do. Eleanor and her mother didn't get along when she was growing up. Her mother was from the old school and felt that children "should be seen, not heard." Since Eleanor had no voice in the matters that affected her, she left home at age seventeen and never returned. Twenty years later her mother still refuses to talk about what happened, referring to Eleanor as "the black sheep." Eleanor, unlike her brother who lives five states away, talks to her mother almost daily and runs errands for her weekly. "It's my daughterly obligation to help my mother out even though we've never been on the same wavelength. She doesn't show her appreciation and I no longer expect it, but she's my mother. It saddens me that we aren't close, but since I don't want to treat her the way she treats me, I choose to do what I can."

Eleanor has been tempted to turn her back and walk away, but instead she's choosing to rise above her hurt and love the best she can. By taking her mother to the grocery store, and to the bank, and by mowing her lawn, Eleanor shows respect for her mother and for herself. She can hold her head up high; her conscience is clear. Some might say she's cleaning up her karma by behaving in a loving manner even though she gets no thanks in return. Eleanor says, "When my mother complains that I am not doing enough, I feel guilty and doubt myself. I struggle with finding the right balance between helping her out and doing what's good for me."

Adult children everywhere show respect for their parents even though they don't always see eye to eye. Most members of the grand generation have mellowed with age. With life experience under their belt, they're able to see the big picture and have gained a larger perspective. They understand where they messed up and have probably changed their ways. By showing respect for your elders, you gain self-respect.

Cherish the Little Ones

The first day of spring I was sitting on a park bench when I saw the most luxurious stroller approach me. Peeking her little head over the edge was the cutest baby wearing a bright red headband. I said to the mother, "Oh, what a cute baby." "Her name is Ruby, she was born on the first day of Spring, and she's one year old today," her mother told me, proudly adding, "She's the most remarkable baby."

"That's exactly the way moms are supposed to be," I thought to myself, "Proud."

My friend Jean likes to look at babies. Whenever we're out and about, she points them out, "Look at that baby with the pink bow," "Oh, look at the little guy with the dimples." Her mother pointed out babies to her, and she did the same with her kids; now she does it with me. "Baby adoration" was ingrained in her from an early age. Just as someone develops an appreciation for all the fine nuances in great music or literature if they're exposed to it and taught to value it as a young child, I guess the same could be said for "baby love."

Jean remembers her mother and father noting almost each and every baby that we would come upon. Their voices would fill with sweetness and delight as they commented on each baby's special charms. "My sister and I could have been a little jealous of my parents' interests in other children, but the nature of the subject left us no other choice but to agree with them, and in turn, I too have passed on this tradition to my children."

Jean has actually gone out of her way to check out a baby. When she hears one "singing" or "gurgling" in the next aisle of a store where she's shopping, she heads straight in that direction. "Why?" I asked. "Just because it gives me joy. I can escape whatever mood I'm in, no matter how depressed, irritated, or hassled, when I look into the face of a baby," Jean answered.

It's true. Babies are so darn cute, aren't they? Each has a special sparkle. It's something innocent, an honest and accessible state that shines forth. A source of sweet laughter, enduringly entertaining to observe; they put a smile on our face and soften our hearts. When a baby is near, the world is wondrous. A baby causes a profound shift of awareness if we allow them to do so. It's easy to get stuck in thinking that it's only the adults who are the teachers. But if you practice baby adoration in your family, you'll discover that babies teach us too.

Babies are bundles of optimism in diapers. They infuse us with a fresh perspective—a new way of looking at life. With each baby comes the chance to protect, nurture, educate, and allow a new generation to become the best that they can be. This is part of the attraction. This is something that should be most precious to mankind. If we treat our youngest citizens as national treasures, our communities will reflect this and be less troubled. That's good for all families.

If Jean has her way, "Baby Adoration" will become a social movement beginning with you. Pay close attention to the youngest in your family, fuss over them, cherish their charms, guide them, watch over them, and protect them.

Honor the In-Be-Tweeners

There are cycles in life when you're an in-be-tweener. You may remember that funny awkward stage when you were no longer a child but not yet an adult. Perhaps you had a dry spell after college graduation when you couldn't find a job in the field you'd prepared for. Perhaps you felt the angst of wanting to be part of a couple, but you knew the person you were dating wasn't the right one. If you're married and wanting a child, you know the feeling that comes with wishing, hoping, and trying to get pregnant. Every age, stage, and phase has its in-be-tween times. You've probably felt its restless tug.

It seems as if overnight you went from childhood to adulthood and now, as head of the household, you have big responsibilities. You're no longer a child, you're not an elder, you're in-be-tween, and some days your not sure you like it. You wonder if you're up to the task and ask yourself, "How did this happen?" "Can I manage it all?" Like other in-be-tweeners, you're doing so much. You have big responsibilities; people are counting on you.

Honor yourself for how far you've come and all that you're doing. You've probably managed to figure out how to unclog the toilet, balance a checkbook, sew buttons and hems, yet it's more difficult to figure out how to take a half an hour for yourself. It's a bold venture to figure out how to take good care of yourself while caring for your loved ones. What might you do to honor yourself?

Give yourself a party for one, and celebrate all that you are. Write a testimonial letter on your own behalf, and keep in a private drawer or journal. Pat yourself on the back, and say to yourself several times each day, "I'm doing well." Buy yourself a bouquet.

Each phase has its special charms and challenges; honor them all. Eleven-year-old Emily said to her mom, "It seems like you liked me best when I was little." "What makes you thing that?" her mom asked. "Because you use to put my school papers on the refrigerator and talk about how cute I was—you don't brag about me anymore." In-be-tween kids need pats on the back too. Even if it seems they don't respond openly, in-be-tweeners like to be fussed over. Comment on the little successes in school or the funny observations they're making. Give a flower for "just being you."

Notice all those in-be-tweeners walking around. Nina, seventy-eight years old, told me that when she goes to the mall or to the grocery store, it's the teenagers that are the most polite, "When they see me walking slowly, they get out of my way, smile, and open doors." Do you have teenagers in your family who could use recognition? Far too many adults are rolling their eyes and making stereotypical comments about how difficult teenagers are. This is not encouraging for them to hear. Like you, they're individuals and deserve acknowledgment for the good efforts they're making. And take good care of yourself when you're in-be-tween, for you won't be there for long.

Strive for Understanding

When you strive to understand, your focus is not on who is right or who is wrong, but on arriving at a heightened understanding where there is no winning and no losing. In a loving family everyone has the right to be understood. Communicating in this way is a more positive and enjoyable way of relating.

Misunderstandings and estrangement among families most often arise out of incomplete communication, hidden meanings, and unspoken assumptions. When you assume that you already know what the other person is going to say, or they assume that they know what you mean without hearing you out, then understanding gets cut off prematurely. It's better to spend more time up front, to make sure you're on the same wavelength, than cutting off and having to go back over things later. Adopting a "Talk, Listen, Understand Policy" saves time and turmoil in the long run. That doesn't mean that you can't take a time out before you reach an understanding. It means that you're dedicated to see what life is like from your loved one's perspective. You can say, "I want to understand, but I need to make this phone call first, then I'll be able to pay close attention."

Seeing the glum look on your face, your husband asks, "Honey, what's wrong?" You answer, "Oh, nothing." If he jumps to the assumption that you don't want to talk, and you jump to the assumption that he doesn't care, you're at a communication dead end.

If your child runs through the house tracking mud, laughing, and slamming doors and you yell, "Stop that!" he won't know exactly what you mean, and you'll put a glitch in your relationship. To understand each other you have to talk and listen for specifics. It may take more effort up front, but you'll gain the pleasure of understanding, which, in turn, leads to greater compatibility and family harmony.

To arrive at understanding follow these guidelines: Be specific, ask for clarification, and don't assume. The understanding that develops between you and the rest of your family when you do these three things, will be a source of comfort for all of you.

The "Talk, Listen, Understand Policy" is the most effective way to build trust and a sense of connection. Good relationships depend on us understanding one another. When family members don't feel understood, they'll feel like outsiders and will look elsewhere for acceptance. But when they know that you're taking the time to try to understand, they'll have the security that comes with belonging. Hearing your mom or pop say, "I want to understand, " is like the telephone; it keeps families plugged in and connected. And remember, just because your related doesn't mean everything is open for discussion. Don't spread rumors about each other. If you talk about your sister behind her back, make sure it's something you'd be willing to say to her face.

Believe in One Another

Spiritually brave parents are respectful toward their children, believing in their goodness, and treating them with more dignity and honor than popular culture suggests. "We believe in you" is their theme; it's woven through the fabric of their relationship. When you believe in your children, you're letting them know that you value the unique people that they are, which in turn gives them the security of knowing they have a place in the world.

Life is sweeter when your family believes in you. Lily, the mother of two, told me, "I believed that my family was my sanctuary. No matter how cold and uncaring the rest of the world, I believed that my family was there for me. It refreshed and nurtured me as a child. No matter how tough my day was at school, I knew I was not without someone who cared. This is the security I want to pass on to my children."

Each year I met with hundreds of children and parents, and I must tell you that the children who are thriving are treated respectfully by their parents. I have seen "disadvantaged" children do better in life than their counterparts with more advantages simply because a parent believed wholeheartedly in them, supported them totally, and held them with high regard.

Recently the American Medical Association published a study that concluded that teenagers who feel loved, understood, and noticed by parents are less likely to use drugs and alcohol, attempt suicide, engage in violence, or become sexually active at a young age.

Believing in your children, trusting in their goodness, supporting them, and helping them out through your words and your actions is the foundation for their success. A knowing wink, an encouraging thumbs-up, a reassuring nod lets them know you believe they can do it. Tell them often, "I'm here for you." When they're struggling about what to do next say to them, "I trust you to make the right choice." Believing in our children is not just giving a phony pat on the back, it's having faith in their goodness separate from what they do. It's seeing their sparkle, proclaiming their light.

You convey your belief in your child by allowing him to save face, preserving his self-respect. Eight-year-old Hank ran into the house, angrily throwing down his books. "What's wrong?" his mother, Lynne, asked. "That stupid, jerky bus driver kicked me and Andy off the bus," he said. Instead of jumping to conclusions and saying, "If you got in trouble you must have deserved it," Lynne listened closely and responded to the humiliation he must have been feeling. "That must have been embarrassing," she said. "You must be really mad." After he ate his snack and lay in front of the television for an hour, Lynne was able to approach him about what happened.

Strong feelings do not disappear just because someone says, "It's not nice to feel that way." Feelings lose their sharp edges when you listen with understanding. When you believe in your child's fundamental goodness, he's able to rise to the occasion and do the right thing.

Reminisce

Reminiscing, passing on your family traditions and legends in daily conversation is an integral part of family life; after all, to you, your family history is more important than world history.

Family stories are meaningful. They inspire, impart values, and entertain us. After we have left our family of origin, we take our stories with us, and they help shape our new nuclear family: "In my family we did it this way." Stories help us through our troublesome transitions: "When my cat died . . . ." Stories help us feel better. They also convey bad news and teach us coping skills.

Family stories have significance and power. Young children like to hear, "When you were a baby . . . ." You can be sure they're listening to what you're saying. "He was wide awake from the minute he was born." "She looks just like her grandma." They also hear you talking with your friends: "He's stubborn just like his dad." Family stories teach us about each other and the world. They let us know where we came from. They shape us, help us discover our identity, understand how we fit into the world. That's why so many adoptive children seek out their biological roots. The more you know where you came from, the more you can see any wounds that might need healing.

Discovering your ancestors gives you perspective. You can understand why your mother does what she does when you know how she grew up. Knowing the truth of where you come from liberates you from your past. When you know the skeletons in your closet, you can speak out about what is unacceptable and make a leap forward. The past cannot be changed, but knowing the truth of the past helps you live more comfortably with the present.

Tell each other stories and reminisce. If you have a ten-year-old, you might begin by sharing what life was like for you when you were ten. Use the same technique if you have a teenager. When you tell your story, you're sharing your experience. The person hearing the story can add their experience and opinion; even if you remember the circumstances slightly differently, it's the feeling that comes with sharing that matters most.

Family stories build your family identity and increase your family esteem. When you tell your story about Great-Grandma's spunk, the picture in the photo album comes to life. Courtship stories, new-baby stories, and crazy distant-relative stories all have meaning. Our stories confirm that no matter how independent we are from one another, we are related and we indeed are a family. Like an inside joke, family stories bring you together. Often only you and members of your clan appreciate the ramifications.

Stay Connected While Apart

A mystical, magical tie keeps you forever linked to your family. Even when you're separated by miles, workdays, circumstances, or misunderstandings, your loved ones need to know how you're doing; they want to stay in touch. Being free of commitments is not satisfying. Being disconnected from family is not the mark of an emancipated adult. As we get older, we begin to recognize that we benefit from keeping people in our lives. People who will be there when we are stressed out, calling in the middle of the night, and bringing us chicken soup.

Make sure your kids have seen where you work so that when you're separated they'll have a picture of where you're going. Being able to reach your spouse at work, making sure the kids know how to get in touch with you, even if you're in the middle of an important business meeting, is reassuring. And, at the end of the day, be sure to have catch-up conversations. Share an incident from your day, and maybe they'll share something that happened to them. Asking, "How was your day?" usually brings a nonanswer of "fine" from a kid, but sharing a funny little something that happened to you will pique their interest and get them thinking about the funny little things in their day.

Family members often go through times when they want to get away from each other, break away, strike out on their own, and cut the apron strings. It usually happens when you haven't come into your own as an individual person that you have to temporarily turn your back (literally in a few cases) on your family to find yourself. If this is your situation, know that you don't have to burn your bridges while you're exploring the other shore. You can remain in contact through cards that say "I'm thinking of you" and phone calls to pass on family news. If you make the effort to stay in touch even during times when you're pulling away, you won't have the anger and guilt that comes with cutting all ties. And if your loved one is pulling away from you, make the effort to stay in touch without invading their territory.

Togetherness is balanced by solitude. If you're a gardener, you know that you have to separate the plants that get too big because if the roots are too bunched up, then none of them thrives. By respecting each other's need for privacy, you can be close but not smothered, connected but not strangled. Every family member needs a private spot, a corner of a room, a treasure box, a diary, or a cozy nook for daydreaming. Privacy is the time for taking care of ourselves and recharging our batteries so that we can interact favorably with others.

Even children need time alone to reflect and get to know themselves. Periodic time-outs are a natural outcome of being a separate person. Putting family first over career, friends, and pastimes doesn't mean you can't take time for yourself. With distance, you see how special your mom is and how much you love your dad. Just take a two-day vacation from your baby and see how quickly you miss her.

Incorporate Silence

According to a *Wall Street Journal* poll, nearly two in five Americans said time is tighter than money. Rushing around from morning to night, its seems, sadly, that many parents and children are operating on survival mode—doing this and that, accomplishing this, checking it off, moving to the next thing. Knowing what's important, but not being able to stop the frantic pace; family life is strangled by the crunch of not enough hours and too much to do.

To make the most of the time that you and your family do spend together, shift your focus from rushing to slowing down by incorporating silent moments into every hour. Taking five-minute silent breaks will help you switch from just getting by to flourishing. Silence focuses your attention on what really matters. When your attention is split between what you're doing and what you wish you could be doing, you feel anxious and family life gets squeezed.

The next time you're driving in the car rushing to an appointment try this calming exercise: Turn off the radio. Blow out "shhhh" loud and long. Repeat this three times. Be aware of your shoulders, neck, and teeth. Are your teeth clenched, is your jaw locked tightly? Wiggle your face and let it be loose. Blow out "shhhh" three more times. Once you've mastered the "shhhh" exercise you can play it with your children when they're wound up. It works well at bedtime too.

Another calming exercise, "Listening for the silence," can be done standing in lines, in waiting rooms, working at a desk. Instead of focusing on the noise around you, listen for the gaps, the silence amid the noise. Put your focus on the spaces in between.

A peaceful family lives in a peaceful home. There needs to be peaceful stillness when each person can spend time alone, reflecting and nonengaged. In a harmonious family, the quietness comes not because of fearful walking on eggshells, but from a calm centeredness.

Sometimes our bodies get so wound up they prevent us from calming down. If that's true in your house, try this "Freeze Game" with your partner and children at the end of the day. Put on dancing music and shake your body for five minutes, stop the music, and freeze for one minute, and then repeat dancing and freezing until twenty minutes have passed. Then lie on the floor and breathe. Focus on the silence.

It's in silence that we find the next step, uncover gems of wisdom, and feel loved. In silence, you say much more than if you're jabbering. Try "Communicating with Silence." The next time your spouse or children are talking, don't jump in. If they're talking directly to you, deliberately wait until they're through. Let silence pass between you for thirty seconds. Look pleasant, smile, and nod. Let another thirty seconds pass and when they've stopped talking respond by looking in their eyes, touching their hands. At first they might think you've gone slightly mad, but they'll get soon accustomed to the ripples of peace running through you.

Respond with Warmth

Have you ever been around parents who seemed distant and aloof? You couldn't put your finger on what it was, but you sensed a coldness in their manner? It wasn't in anything they said or did. In fact, at first you were unsure of what you were sensing because they were super polite and said the right thing. Yet they were unapproachable, removed, uptight, and kept their children at arm's length. It was as if they'd cut themselves off, tightly closed down their hearts. Instead of being open and warm, they'd become hard, cold, and aloof. Something was missing, and you felt sad for them and their children.

Warmth is a healing vibration felt by you and the person on the receiving end. It's a quality of compassion, kindness; it's joy in living. Warmth is a feeling of tenderness. When you respond with warmth toward your family, they become less defensive; fears melt away.

Warmth is a generosity of spirit. It means being willing to give the best slice of pizza, the best steak, or the last piece of cake. It means not asking "What's in it for me?" but rather "What can I do for you?" It's about not controlling, not blaming, and not keeping score. Responding with warmth and kindness is good family manners. It's infectious. Parents who respond with warmth to the needs of their children bring up respectful adults who in turn are responsive to their parents.

Responding with warmth means a soft look in your eye, a pleasant smile on your face. It's noticing the look on your loved one's face that says "I'm having a bad day" and asking: "Is there anything I can do?" It's taking a moment to make his lunch, to start her bath. It's lending a hand to your son as he struggles to clean up his room. It's being empathetic: "Tell me what happened."

No matter how difficult or troubled your family life might be, there are things you can do that will improve your relationships immediately. It doesn't require much time or take much effort to respond to your loved one with warmth, but it does so much good. Ask, "How was your day?" Acknowledge their efforts: "I appreciate you wiping up the counter." The little niceties have lasting consequences: "Thank you, honey." "I'm sorry." "I see what you mean." "Help me, I'd like to understand." Responding with warmth keeps your relationship moving in a positive direction. Warmth allows love to flow from you toward your family, allows the lines of communication to open up, and allows the walls of mistrust to dissolve.

Do No Harm

If you grew up in a family that didn't value its members, you know what a daunting task it can be to overcome the residue of self-doubt you have inherited. If your family didn't value family life, you know the longing for a comforting connection. If, as a child, your family life was troubled or tormented, you know the challenge of defeating shame and guilt.

You can't change what happened to you in the past, but you can stop the cycle from continuing. Right now, you can stop the crippling legacy by pledging: "I will do no harm." What does it mean to do no harm? It means facing the dark side of family life squarely, looking at it directly so that you're no longer ambushed, fooled, or blinded. There is a dark side to family life, and if you've tasted it, you know that the battle is now inside of you. The battle to "do no harm" always begins as an inside job—as a struggle to free ourselves from self-deception. For it is through self-examination that we heal.

Children are the most vulnerable in our families and in our society. As a result they're the victims of the greatest evil; they're inflicted with the greatest harm. Damage sneaks in wearing many disguises. Scape-goating—blaming children for what is the adults' fault—wreaks havoc in families. Instead of facing their own dark tendencies, adults project them onto children. This saps a child's spirit, kills her God-given liveliness. Thousands of children are labeled as troubled and taken to counselors by parents who say "Fix him." The source of the problem however, is not within the child but rather within the parent, the family, the school, or society. If you're a parent of a troubled child, there is something inside of you that needs healing. Behavioral patterns are handed down from generation to generation. Victims of abuse grow up to inflict the same abuse on their own children, often in more subtle forms, unless they've taken the initiative to do no more harm. Don't make your child the recipient of your own unhealed wounds.

If you were mistreated as a child, the right thing to do is to admit it so that you can recognize hidden tendencies and patterns. With the support of a wise person, perhaps a trained counselor, you can make life-affirming choices and stop the harm that was inflicted on you from continuing. With new awareness you have choice and can choose to behave differently. With the help of a wise person, examining your own heart will bring healing and restore goodness.

Touch Only with Love

Touching should never be used to discipline. If you handle your children harshly with hands or fists or if you use brute force to overpower them, they'll wrap invisible armor around their bodies, souls, and psyches. Eventually they won't get much joy out of physical contact. They won't come to you and won't trust you any longer. Physical harshness—hitting, slapping, pinching, thumping, twisting, yanking—is not only inappropriate, unnecessary, and unproductive, it's torture and creates enormous pain and long-standing problems. Sexual touching between adult and child is taboo in cultures around the world because of the deep wounds and unspeakable confusion it creates. It's wrong to tell your family that you love them and then hurt them by your touch.

Touching should be always be soft and reassuring. Hailey couldn't get the words out to tell her father what was wrong, she couldn't stop crying, but when Dad put his reassuring hand on her shoulder, she calmed down enough to tell him what had happened. Your child naturally unwinds when you touch him softly.

Cuddling, hugging, gently holding hands, and walking arm and arm is comforting for body and soul. When the blues come upon you, when you're upset and frustrated, when you're disappointed, or when you're feeling "little," a soft embrace, a silent nod, or a gentle look soothes better than advice. A reassuring hand on your back and a warm embrace, like a fresh breeze, comforts the senses in ways that words never can. Pent-up tension melts away; you relax and catch your breath.

Healing touch arises from a compassionate heart and extends itself in kindness. Don't come down hard on your sweet ones—don't hit, slap, or spank. Gentle touch radiates rejuvenating energy and expresses your concern. If your daughter is crying, be patient and understanding, you don't want to make her feel ashamed. If your son is gloomy and isn't up to talking, don't force. If he doesn't want a hug, don't intrude. Respect his desire for distance yet stay close by so that he knows you care. When he's relaxed once again, you can reach out gently.

Loving touch is the preventative salve between you and your family. There are simple ways to incorporate more touch. Fussy babies fall asleep when rocked and held by a calm parent; wives melt in the arms of a protective, sensitive husband; husbands relax with a foot or shoulder massage; and grandparents get goosebumps when hugged by a child. Try giving each other a hand and finger massage or rub each others' head and temples. Claire couldn't get her wound-up five-year-old to fall asleep at night until she discovered the magic of a nightly back massage. Claire said, "Now my five-year-old not only looks forward to going to bed, she's out like a light."

When you touch each other gently, you'll not only be connected, your family will be mellow.

Lift Each Other Up

Every time you and your family come together, each of you has an experience that you will take with you for the rest of your life. What do you want that experience to be? The spiritual purpose of a family is to lift each other up, raise our spirits, enhance our well-being, and exalt our souls. You know you've had a meaningful family gathering, a peak encounter, when you come away enriched, feeling high. Not just on a superficial high, not just pumped up by feel-good cover-ups, but deeply satisfied.

Always rejoice in the good fortune of your brother or your sister. If your sister gets a new house, a fancy car, and a handsome husband, while you have nothing, be happy for her. If you're envious, say: "I'm happy for you even though I'm envious." She'll respect your honesty and admire your generosity of heart. It's human nature to be covetous, but don't put your energy into bad-mouthing her.

Don't waste your energies comparing yourself to her. Your destinies are different, yet your paths have crossed for a reason. Staying stuck in envy, jealousy, or greed pulls you down and makes you bitter, stingy, and selfish. Congratulate your brother and your sister for their efforts and successes. By offering your best wishes you immediately rise above any egotistical tendencies.

Whatever good happens to you, immediately share it. Don't hoard your good fortune. Stockpiling your riches makes you a miser. Don't cover up your joy or enthusiasm. Hiding your light makes you feel dark inside. Sharing your blessings sheds gladness on all of you. If your brother has never invited you to his home for a meal, don't get caught up in getting even. Instead, invite him over, smile, and serve him dinner. Send your cousin a "Thinking of You" card, and write a few sentences about what you shared as children. If your grandparents, aunts, or uncles don't acknowledge what you've given or give back to you, still trust in the divine order of life. Remember that the more you share, the more treasures come back to you in unknown ways from unknown sources. There are plenty of opportunities to get pushed around, ignored, and torn down by strangers, you don't need to add hostilities by behaving badly toward your brother, sister, or extended family members.

Some folks say they can be generous when the mortgage is paid, when they have a new car, when the kids are off to college, or when there's enough money in savings. Happiness is an inner spiritual state that has nothing to do with material possessions. Knowing that you're loved and behaving lovingly is the source of happiness, peace, and contentment. Don't wait until you're dying to say, "I love you." Show your family members compassion before they are gone. You create misunderstandings by ignoring each other. Use every opportunity instead to lift each other up.

Give Lasting Gifts

Cindy, the second oldest of four siblings, said to her sister, "You're Mom's favorite." "No, I'm not," Susan insisted; "She likes the boys best." "Well, you're her favorite daughter," claimed Cindy.

It wasn't the first time Sharon, their mom, had overheard the "Mom likes you best" conversation. Over the years, the kids squabbled openly about who was Mom's favorite. The boys were convinced that she liked girls best, and each girl maintained that whomever she preferred, it was someone other than herself. Sharon couldn't remember how many times she'd explained that a mother loves all of her children equally, so this time she approached the argument from a slightly different angle. She composed four individual letters that began, "You are my favorite child because . . . ." and then listed their special characteristics—"your sense of humor, your enthusiasm, your determination, your good nature"—each letter elaborating on the uniqueness of each one. Placing the finished letter on each pillow, she crossed her fingers hoping they'd understand. It worked; the letters transformed the bickering. Twelve years later, the four, now grown, are planning to one day write, "You're my favorite because" letters to their own children.

Presents are great to give and receive. Unwrapping one, you feel adored. Even though Granddad Harry lived in the same city, he sent packages in the mail wrapped with so much tape and string that it took the grandkids a very long time to reach inside. The gifts were nothing special, but boy did the kids love receiving them! Gifts are testimonies to the specialness between you, mementos of big and little occasions. Give as many as you want, as often as you like, but make sure that some of the gifts are the lasting kind.

Mary decorated twelve loose-leaf binders, filled them with recipes for the family's favorite dishes, and gave the cookbooks for Christmas one year. Arthur gave his sixty-eight-year-old father piano lessons. Marty gave her husband framed baby pictures of the two of them. Carl gave his wife a date each week for a year.

Whether it's lessons, letters, or the gift of time, tie the gift to your values and situation. If you emphasize only material possessions or the price of the gift, you're likely to feel bankrupt. Even if you're wealthy right now, fortunes change. Until the divorce, Sandi bought whatever she wanted, but now she has to economize. Her daughters are good sports even though they'd rather have designer shoes and jeans. Sandi tells them, "If I had a money tree, I'd buy them for you." Since she doesn't, they're learning about nonmaterial gifts—beauty in nature, a happy experience, the abundance of friendship, a shoulder to cry on, the value of spending time with each other. "We talk about how rich we are even though we don't have extra money," they say.

When Olivia, who describes herself as a "family of one," turned thirty, she threw herself a "secondhand party." On the invitations to neighbors and friends she wrote, "Secondhand, recycled, or handmade gifts only."

Lasting gifts might be mementos or heirlooms, trinkets or baubles. They can be expensive, cheap, handmade, or free. What determines whether it's lasting or not isn't the size or the price, but rather the thought and care you put in it, and that you give it sincerely.

Find Your Spiritual Footing

Your duty as a parent has sacred importance. Not only are you teaching your child how to survive in the world and how to relate to others, you're teaching by your example the great spiritual principals. For it's in your family that you learn how to love others and how to be a good human being—the essence of all spiritual teachings. With a spiritual footing, your child begins to understand that life has meaning and purpose. It's your holy obligation to raise your children well by providing a context for their spiritual growth.

All individuals within your family have spiritual needs, which vary according to age and level of understanding. From birth to six years old, a child is learning to trust and feel safe. Can he trust you to meet his needs for food, shelter, safety, and security? He's helpless to take care of himself, but when he knows that he can trust you to be there for him, as he matures, he's able to place his trust in the Divine. Perhaps you might talk with your little ones about angels watching over or read bedtime stories about nature spirits. Kids understand that there are happy invisible creatures dancing all around us. Say prayers of gratitude together each day. Sing cheerful songs of praise.

As your child's level of understanding develops, there are countless opportunities to discuss the spiritual side of life. If a family pet dies, you can talk about the animal's spirit living on in your heart. When our gold-fish died, six-year-old Amanda and I held a funeral. It was a big event, and she invited the neighborhood kids. We buried Goldie in a little box under a tree. I used the opportunity to talk about how the soul leaves the body and lives forever. We laughed about the fish's special qualities, and Amanda wrote on a rock, "Here lies a very good fish." I felt good about the experience, as she was more prepared when she attended her grandpa's funeral a few years later.

As children attend school, they become aware of religious traditions other than their own. If you're Christian, you might talk about the Jewish or Hindu traditions so that they understand that there are many spiritual paths. Teenagers are looking for excitement; they want to explore the world. Colin took a yoga class at the gym, saw a movie on Tibet, and began reading about Buddhism. Claire used this opportunity to discuss life's essential questions with her son—Who am I? Where am I going? What is my purpose? When your child has a disappointment, talk about the spiritual reality that may not be obvious to the untrained eye. Tell her "when one door closes, another door opens." Share an experience of this truth from your life.

As you mature, you become increasingly aware of the longings of your soul. A spiritual footing is more than attending church once a week; it's bringing sacredness into everyday life. It's being aware of our doubts and searching for the answers. A spiritual footing gives us peace about things we don't fully understand. It motivates us to right the wrongs and reach out to those who are suffering. It's about bringing faith into the daily grind and knowing that all things are working for good and that behind every cloud there's a silver lining.

Simplify to Be Together

Implanted in the heart of each of us is the aspiration to be part of a loving family. We want it, we know we need it, yet our lives get so complicated that we overlook the simple moments that together add up to quality family life.

Ask yourself this question: What do I need to do to improve my relationship with my spouse or with my child? Listen to your answer, then follow your own advice. Over the years, I have asked parents and couples this question and I can only remember a handful of people who didn't have an answer. Almost all the people I've asked have known what they needed to do. Their answers were delightfully simple, straightforward, and doable. Most people said uncomplicated things such as "play catch with my son," "hold hands with my wife," "talk less and listen more," "read to my daughter." One man told me, "I'd be a better dad and husband if I worked less overtime and just went home."

Quality time with your family doesn't have to be prearranged or elaborate. Often the best quality time is spontaneous. It's putting the newspaper aside to play checkers on the floor with your four-year-old. It's sitting in the bleachers during swim team practice, it's being the Scout leader because it's important to your child, it's bringing your wife a rose and telling her she's pretty, and serving your husband his favorite dessert.

Spend one-on-one time with each of your children and partner. Empty your mind of distractions so you can be with them in the moment. Shift your attention from outside obligations so you can really be present. After all, what good is time together if you're preoccupied?

Simplifying now brings lasting rewards. In years to come you'll have the glow of satisfaction knowing that you made room in your day for them. Your children will look back and remember too. The moments you spent together will give them eternal reassurance that they were loved. When you're reviewing your life, these moments will be your treasure.

In Puerta Vallarta on Sunday evenings, extended families of grandparents, moms, dads, and children dress in their finery and walk the Malacon. I don't know for sure if they are enjoying themselves, but to an outsider looking on, it sure looks grand. Next time the moon is full, surprise your loved ones by inviting them for a moonlight stroll.

Celebrate Precious Moments

Family life is chock full of stages, phases, rites of passage, traditions, and plenty of "firsts": First birthday, first steps, first tooth, first grade, first braid, first bike, first job, first date, first dance, first anniversary, first whiskers, first gray hairs. With applause and bountiful kudos, ordinary moments are filled with celebration: "That was a first for you today wasn't it, honey?" "Those garlic potatoes you made for dinner were fabulous." "Todd learned his times tables at school today."

The quality of your family life is directly affected by the moments you celebrate. It's the little things, the precious moments, the firsts as well as the traditions, that together add up to a rich family life. Although it might seem that family life is boring, if you look closely you'll discover its freshness. When you begin to notice the ordinary things, family life is a festival of newness: the look on your child's face as he slides down the slide, the tears of pride at your daughter's recital, the glow that washes through you when you hold one another tight, the pillow talk late at night.

Precious moments come and go in a twinkling. Notice it all, take it all in, so that you won't be caught with the regret of taking each other for granted, or be left wondering where the time went. Go for a walk at the first snowfall, point out the buds of spring, hang a summer banner from the front door the very day that school lets out, and decorate your kitchen counter with fall leaves and pumpkins.

Mia and Mark had been married twenty-seven hours when a misunderstanding led to a tiff. Mia cried, and Mark went for a walk. They don't remember what the fuss was all about because an hour later Mark returned and said, "We just had our first married fight, can we do our first married makeup?"

The wheel of family life is turning, moving, going forward. Beginning with birth and continuing through death, predictable ceremonies and family traditions underline the journey, giving you a sense of continuity and belonging. There are plenty of big happenings where you can pull out all the stops and have a wingding: You earned a promotion, you've been married twenty-five years, the braces are paid for and are coming off, the kids are graduating, Grandma turns seventy-five. There are sentimental moments where a song and toast is the perfect benediction. When Grandpa Gino died, his wife, children, grandchildren, extended clan of brothers, cousins, and old cronies gathered for the wake. There were plenty of tears, reminiscing, eating, and drinking. His granddaughter Francesca sang his favorite song, "That's Amore," and his oldest son, Tony, gave the toast: "Here's to Gino, the man who lived on purpose."

It doesn't matter if you celebrate with a candle, a cake, or a speech, what matters is that you acknowledge the moments that constitute your family life. All the beginnings and all the endings, the biggest accomplishments, the tedious tasks, the smallest virtues—recognize them all, honor them well.

Provide a Loving Presence

"If you don't shape up this minute, I'm running away to the seashore." "If you don't get your chores done, I'll drive you all to boot camp." "Who do you think I am, your servant or your father?" "You kids are driving me to the funny farm."—I have heard Nick, a single father, make these outrageous statements and others like them to his three children on many occasions. His brash pronouncements might be shocking, except that he says them with such good humor and tenderness that his kids, giggling and squirming with delight, get up and do as they're told.

I'm sure you've been in the grocery store or other public place, and overheard a parent cussing out a child or a companion. If the words weren't profane, the tone was. The look on their face was enough to frighten cats. You may have wanted to interrupt and ask them why they were using that tone, why they looked so mean. You wondered to yourself why were they saying such hurtful things to the person who was the most important. Why were they saving polite conversation and manners for other people?

A loving family lifts you up, inspires you, soothes your wounds, sets you straight, tries to understand even when they don't. It's the caring for one another that makes a family, regardless of its composition. A family is where we soothe our aches, heal our bruised souls, laugh, and get things done.

What children need most are happy, conscious parents—parents who know that when they most want to hit their child is the time to hug him. Parents who treat the most important people in their life as though they are. Parents who never give up.

The Nyguen family, refugees from Vietnam, wrote on their annual Christmas card, "Our little family is at peace with the world. I guess that's all I can strive for—moment to moment, day to day—to stay peaceful within myself so that it radiates outwardly to the rest of my family and the people I come in contact with."

When in doubt about what to do, how to behave, what action to take, always provide a loving presence. Experiment with love. Find as many ways as possible to help each other and have fun. Live in the present. You don't have to be an expert in parenting, you don't have to know all there is about relationships, simply treat your child and spouse they way you want them to treat you.

Be Grateful for Your Lessons

A family, like an orchestra, is made up individuals, each playing an important part. In a symphony it would be ridiculous if the conductor insisted that the bass be like the violin and that the violin be like the cello. It also would be silly if the orchestra always played the same piece. Your family's composition, like that of a great orchestra, is always in motion. You move from one position to the other—conductor, solo, and duet. Once you were a daughter, now you have a daughter, someday you may have a granddaughter.

The family of your dreams may not match with your reality. Perhaps you live in a blended family or a stepfamily. Perhaps someone in your family has special needs. Maria and Darin, anticipating the arrival of their first baby, were filled with great excitement. Merriment filled their home as they made all the usual preparations; reading baby books, decorating the nursery, going over lists of names, dreaming of a happy threesome. Janae, weighing 5 lbs 12 oz, was born at 5:00 p.m. on a Saturday. Maria and Darin didn't know anything was out of the ordinary at first. When they were told, they were in shock—they'd expected everything to be fine. They were in grief—they'd envisioned something different and now all their fantasies were gone. Maria called friends and family and through her tears said, "We had our baby—a little girl. She has Down Syndrome." Right away, Maria and Darin had to deal with many things they weren't prepared for, things they knew nothing about—special feedings, heart surgery, insurance companies. From the beginning, they fought for their baby's rights. "How do they do it?" bystanders wondered. It wasn't easy, but they did it by focusing on the love they felt for their daughter and putting their energies into moving heaven and earth for this precious child.

Your family will not fulfill your every longing, but because of these people, you are who you are. Haven't they all helped you in a certain way? Even the worst family scenario has something to be thankful for. The wife who left you, the parents who abandoned you, the husband who ran away with someone else—everything is moving toward good. Dark nights are the backdrop for a beautiful morning.

Your children are your greatest teachers. Getting up in the middle of night to care for your sick child, didn't you learn about yourself? Even though your parents may have been inadequate, perhaps even cruel, they were also your teachers.

The authentic mother and father focus on what they have, not on what's missing. Appreciate everything, especially the mundane routine, the ordinary events of day-to-day family life. For, when you appreciate the ordinary you click into the joy.

Be grateful for all of life—the stars, the moon, the trees, your parents, your brothers and sisters, your blessed children. You didn't earn them—they were given to you. When you feel grateful, you'll discover that you can't feel grateful enough. You cannot repay, but you can be grateful. It's through gratitude that your family is united.

About the Author

JUDY FORD, L.C.S.W., a nationally recognized family therapist, educator, and bestselling author, has dedicated her life to family healing and wholeness. She has worked for nearly three decades with children and families in various settings—from gang turf in the inner city to crisis intervention in hospitals. Her workshops, "Parenting with Love and Laughter" and "Gentle Discipline," have been attended by thousands. Articles about her work have appeared in numerous publications, including *Family Circle, Good Housekeeping,* and *Women's World.* She has appeared on *Oprah!* and CNN, and has also been interviewed on National Public Radio. A family therapist, she resides in Washington state.

Workshop and speaking information is available at Judy's Web site: *www.judyford.com* or you may email: *judy@judyford.com*

photograph by Amanda Ford

To Our Readers

Conari Press, an imprint of Red Wheel/Weiser, publishes books on topics ranging from spirituality, personal growth, and relationships to women's issues, parenting, and social issues. Our mission is to publish quality books that will make a difference in people's lives—how we feel about ourselves and how we relate to one another. We value integrity, compassion, and receptivity, both in the books we publish and in the way we do business.

Our readers are our most important resource, and we value your input, suggestions, and ideas about what you would like to see published. Please feel free to contact us, to request our latest book catalog, or to be added to our mailing list.

Conari Press
An imprint of Red Wheel/Weiser, LLC
500 Third Street, Suite 230
San Francisco, CA 94107
www.redwheelweiser.com